Praise for Patrick F. McManus

"When you start one of McManus's short stories, you just never know where you're going to land; all you know for certain is that you're going to chuckle."

—*Outdoor Life*

"What a treat to come across a Patrick McManus tale."

—*Los Angeles Times*

"[*Kerplunk!*] comes at you harmlessly enough, but soon has you holding your gut and wiping the tears from your eyes."

—Brett Prettyman, *The Salt Lake Tribune*

"The funniest writer around today."

—*The Atlanta Journal-Constitution*

"McManus narrates his woodsy stories with a laid-back style that will earn many smiles of fond recognition from anyone who's heard a guide say, 'I know there used to be a trail here.'"

—*Publishers Weekly*

"Readers familiar with McManus' writings will sink right in, grinning before they even crack open the book, and newcomers will find themselves seized with a compulsion to read the rest of McManus' numerous compilations."

—*Booklist*

Also by Patrick F. McManus

Kerplunk!
STORIES

PATRICK F. MCMANUS

SIMON & SCHUSTER PAPERBACKS

New York   London   Toronto   Sydney

SIMON & SCHUSTER PAPERBACKS
1230 Avenue of the Americas
New York, NY 10020

Copyright © 2007 by Patrick F. McManus

All rights reserved, including the right to reproduce this book or
portions thereof in any form whatsoever. For information address
Simon & Schuster Subsidiary Rights Department, 1230 Avenue of the
Americas, New York, NY 10020

First Simon & Schuster trade paperback edition November 2008

SIMON & SCHUSTER PAPERBACKS and colophon are registered
trademarks of Simon & Schuster, Inc.

For information about special discounts for bulk purchases,
please contact Simon & Schuster Special Sales at
1-800-456-6798 or business@simonandschuster.com.

DESIGNED BY KATE MOLL

Manufactured in the United States of America

13 15 17 19 20 18 16 14 12

The Library of Congress has cataloged the hardcover edition as follows:

McManus, Patrick F.
Kerplunk! : stories / Patrick F. McManus.
p. cm.
1. American wit and humor. I. Title.
PN6165.M395 2007
818'.5402—dc22   2007008107
ISBN-13: 978-0-7432-8049-5
ISBN-10:   0-7432-8049-0
ISBN-13: 978-0-7432-8050-1 (pbk)
ISBN-10:   0-7432-8050-4 (pbk)

See page 229 for full information on where
these stories originally appeared.

To Dave Lisaius,
for all the great adventures
and his superb comic spirit!

Contents

Kerplunk!

The first advice I ever received about fishing was passed on by a teenage ranch hand when I was six years old. As often happened in those days, a spontaneous card party had erupted at the main ranch house one Sunday afternoon, and it was decided by the rancher that everyone should stay for dinner that evening. The fact that the ranch larder had little on hand to feed twenty or so people bothered the rancher not at all. He simply turned to one of the older boys and ordered, "Biff, go catch us some fish for supper."

To my mind, this was about the same as ordering up a miracle: "Biff, go to the moon and back before supper." My own father, a member of the card party, probably reacted to the order about the same as I did. Dad didn't put on any airs that he was some kind of sportsman, but catching a fish for him was about equal in difficulty to working out the mathematics for Einstein's theory of relativity. (I inherited my father's genes for both mathematics and fishing.)

Although Biff didn't seem particularly pleased with this assignment, he turned to me and said, "C'mon, Pat, I'll show you how to catch fish."

It must have been in the spring of the year, March or April, because I recall great, greasy masses of frog eggs in pools of water scattered about the meadow through which the creek meandered. I never did see the actual creek, because it was bordered on both sides by brush considerably higher than Biff's head.

The fish-catching apparatus apparently was well established at the ranch. Biff stopped by one of the barns and scooped large handfuls of worms out of a box of soil. He put the worms in a rusty can and the can in an old milk bucket. Then we headed out into the watery meadow. Biff hadn't bothered with a fishing rod, and I soon discovered why.

Leaning up against the brush along the creek every ten yards or so was a slender, peeled tamarack pole. Each was about ten feet long. A line ran from the tip to the butt. A heavy lead sinker was attached to the line. A sturdy leader ran from the line to the hook. The hook was neatly tucked into the butt of the pole. (Please note that I do not dignify these contraptions by referring to them as "rods.")

Biff undid a hook and placed a bit of worm on it. He then whipped the pole around in a rather graceful arc and sent hook, line, and sinker flying over the brush. (This action was much more difficult to accomplish than it seemed, as I was shortly to find out.) It was then that I received my first bit of fishing advice.

"Always listen for the kerplunk," Biff said.

"The kerplunk?" I said.

"Yeah," he said. "*Kerplunk* is the sound your sinker makes hitting the water. If you don't hear the kerplunk, your hook may be sitting on a log or hung up on the brush. Your line's not even in the water."

I have remembered that bit of fishing advice all my life and follow it even to this day whenever I am in a situation that requires me to hurl a baited hook over a wall of brush. Indeed, it is good advice for everyday life: Always listen for the kerplunk. Otherwise, your line may not even be in the water.

As I recall, the catching of the fish that day was rather tedious and miserable, the weather being wet and cold. Biff baited the hook on each pole, and then whipped the line over the brush. We then walked back to the beginning of the row of poles—I think there were eight or ten of them—and, reversing his maneuver of sending the line out over the brush, he brought it back, with a fish looping through the air and plopping on the ground behind us. Most of the trout we caught seemed to run to the small side, about eight inches or so. (Good, though!) Biff dropped each in the bucket as he caught it. Within an hour and a half we had in the bucket what in those days was described quite accurately as "one heck of a mess of fish." Still, I doubt we were over our combined limit, because the limit for trout back then was twenty-one per fisherman. So we would have been perfectly legal, provided Biff had had a license.

I think the unofficial limit back then was "all you can catch plus one fish," but even so it was unusual for anyone to reach even the official limit. To say you caught your limit meant something in those days. It usually meant you were lying.

I remember only one fellow back then who practiced catch-and-release. He was eventually nabbed, I think, and placed in an institution.

Biff also gave me my second piece of fishing advice: Use a strong leader. I doubt his own leaders could have been used to tow a logging truck out of a mud hole, but they would have served well for most jobs short of that. As I mentioned earlier, I found casting a line over the wall of brush to be much harder than it looked. Several times I cast over the brush and didn't hear the kerplunk on the other side. On these occasions Biff would drag the log or stump or branch or whatever the hook had become attached to back over the brush. Also, I don't recall ever losing a fish because a leader snapped off. So always remember to use a strong leader, particularly if you're fishing with a tamarack pole.

I started fishing with flies when I was about ten. Later I would learn there is nothing that attracts unwanted advice so voluminously as fly-fishing, but back then my fishing buddy, one Vern Schulze, didn't know any more about fly-fishing than I did.

If Vern caught a fish, I'd ask him, "What are you using?"

"A big old gray thing with white wings," he'd reply.

"Good," I'd say. "I've got one of those."

There were two flies we actually knew the names of: Black Gnat and Royal Coachman. If someone asked us what our favorite fly was, however, we'd almost always say Royal Coachman, because that sounded so much better than Black Gnat. Neither of us ever caught a fish on the Royal Coachman. Apparently, the fish in our part of the country had never seen a bug that looked even remotely like a Royal Coachman.

All of our flies were big, too: #10s, and even #8s and #6s. You needed hooks that big in order to get a really strong leader to fit through the eyes. But we seldom lost a fly. Oh, sure, sometimes, when we had to drag a stump or log out of a creek, but it was better than losing a fly.

I've fished with Vern for more than half a century, and I don't think he has even once given me a bit of advice on how to catch fish. He always catches more fish than I do, so maybe it's just that he doesn't want to reveal any of his secrets.

Our method of fly-fishing was, first, get the fly in the water. That's it, there's nothing else: Get the fly in the water. If the fly isn't in the water, it isn't going to catch a fish. Even though I have two whole library shelves devoted to fly-fishing, the entirety of my fly-fishing technique, after all these years, consists of nothing more than getting the fly in the water. This fact raises great consternation among my fly-fishing friends and guides. They cannot help but shout advice to me, occasionally with the emphasis of very bad fourteen-letter words. "Keep your rod tip up!" they shout. "Keep the rod tip down! Keep that fish away from the boat! Don't let it get under the boat! Put some goop on your line! Put some goop on your fly! Cast over there! Cast over here! Pump! Pump! Mend your line!"

My fly casting has been compared by a guide to having the exact same motions as those of an old lady fighting off a bee with a broom handle. I thought that was particularly cruel. One guide even complained that he was afraid my casting was going to upset the boat. Yeah, well, anyone who puts a 5-weight line on a 7-weight rod will cast like that. Try it yourself.

My response to most of the advice and criticism hurled at my fishing technique is to smile and nod, as though I have just absorbed some great truth. Then I will turn and say, very soberly, "But remember this one thing. Always listen for the kerplunk."

You see, I know a great many people who have never heard a kerplunk, and therefore never even realize they don't have their line in the water.

The Art of Trailering

Back in 1952, **a** guy by the name of Milo Psinsky hooked up a trailer to his car, and all the trailer lights worked. Milo was briefly considered for sainthood, but, alas, sainthood required two miracles instead of just one.

Outdoorsmen are about the only people nowadays who still use trailers—utility, mountain bike, snowmobile, boat, and camping. At the moment, I am down to only three trailers: two boat and one utility/camping. The lights don't work properly on any of the three. That doesn't bother me too much, because I know that is the nature of trailer lights.

A highway patrolman stopped me recently and told me that my boat-trailer signal light had indicated a left turn, and I had made a right turn.

"What's your point?" I said.

"I just thought you might be interested," he said. "I have a boat trailer that does the same thing."

"The turn signals on all boat trailers work that way," I said. "If you see a trailer signaling left, you know the driver is going to make a right turn. It's practically a law of physics."

"Really?" he said. "I didn't know that. Here's a ticket."

I'm not sure if trailer lights are still a major cause for divorce in this country. I believe that was the case at one time, when trailers were in common use. The grounds for divorce developed like this. The husband hooks up a trailer, and of course the lights don't work. Typically, there are four wires: yellow, green, brown, and white. If there are more than four wires, you should immediately walk away from the trailer and call either a mechanic or a bomb-disposal unit. People have been institutionalized after attempting to hook up trailer lights with more than four wires.

Now, even though there are only four wires involved, the number of combinations in which the wires from the car can be connected to the wires from the trailer is somewhere in the neighborhood of 4,500. To find the right combination, one simply employs the process of elimination. Typically, the right combination turns out to be number 4,499.

The process of elimination requires two people, typically a husband and wife. The wife is usually the one stationed behind the trailer, in the position of observer. The husband either crouches or lies on his back near the respective light plugs of the vehicle and trailer. He begins working his way through the various combinations of wire connections.

"Okay," he shouts to his wife. "Did the left rear signal light go on?"

"No," she replies. "But the right rear signal light went on."

The man mutters something under his breath, and then shouts, "Is the left light blinking now?"

"No," she shouts back. "But the right rear brake light went on."

They continue in this manner for a couple of hours, by which time the husband begins to suspect that his wife is lying to him, out of sheer malice, about which light went on. Soon they degenerate into name-calling and eventually end up in divorce court. Trailer lights are not to be taken lightly.

The first trailer I ever bought had been fashioned by a backyard madman out of the rusty rear half of a pickup truck. He had painted it blue, with house paint. It was not attractive. Still, I figured it might work as a camping trailer. The madman I bought the trailer from was not the madman who had built it. He was a different madman. I was the madman who tried to get a license for it.

"What's the ID number of the trailer?" the licensing lady asked me.

"It doesn't have one," I said.

"Who was the manufacturer?"

"Milo Psinsky," I said.

The lady said she couldn't give me a license for a trailer built by Milo Psinsky. Every time I went back to the courthouse to license the trailer, I got the same lady. She seemed to enjoy my torment and perhaps thought she could keep her ruse going for another four or five years. Then one day I went into the courthouse and got another lady. She had me sign a couple of forms, and gave me a trailer license.

"Do you know how to fix trailer lights, too?" I asked her.

"No," she said. "Neither did my ex-husband, the fool."

Many people have trouble backing up trailers. The procedure is really quite easy. Simply remember this bit of advice: You put your hand on the bottom of the steering wheel, then move your hand in the direction you want the trailer to turn. Or maybe you put your hand on the top of the steering wheel. I think it's the top. No, wait, it's the bottom. I'm sure it's the bottom. The main thing is to pay attention to what you are doing while backing up. Ignore all crunching sounds and people who are screaming at you. Remember to remain calm.

There are some show-offs who like to back up their trailers with a bit of flair. One day while I was waiting to launch my boat at a Puget Sound ramp, a show-off whipped his pickup truck around and backed his boat trailer down the ramp. I should mention that his pickup truck probably cost more than my house. His boat was almost as big as my house. The maneuver was so quickly and expertly done, I developed an instant hatred for the guy. His boat slid effortlessly off the trailer and floated up against the dock. He had two beautiful, bikini-clad babes with him, whose function, I believe, was to hold the boat against the dock while he parked his pickup. The man then roared back up the ramp—with his boat bouncing along behind him. He had forgotten to untie his boat's bowline from the trailer! Ha! His mishap produced smiles all along the line of us boaters waiting to launch. That, of course, was before we realized how long it takes to remove a large boat that has been dragged halfway up the only launch ramp.

Trailer hitches are basically pretty simple affairs, at least if you have a modicum of mechanical skills and knowledge. My hitch, for example, has a ball-like doohickey bolted onto a steel whatsis about a foot long. You slide the whatsis into a whatchamacallit under the middle of your rear bumper. Then you line up the holes in the whatsis and whatchamacallit, respectively—this takes scarcely more than an hour or two—and then you shove a thingamajig through the aligned holes and fasten it in with a zimp, simple as that.

A word of caution: The clamplike thing that is supposed to go over the doohickey and connect the trailer to the towing vehicle, well, sometimes this won't go over the doohickey. That's because the doohickey is too big for the trailer hitch.

You have the wrong size doohickey bolted to the whatsis that goes into the whatchamacallit. This is not a rare occurrence. In fact, if you happen to have several trailers of different sizes, as I do, it will happen 98 percent of the time. Change the doohickey to the proper size. Do not—I repeat, do not—jump up and down on the trailer tongue in an effort to make the hitch parts connect. It won't work. Take my word for it.

Also, always fasten your safety chains securely to the towing vehicle. This will prevent your trailer and boat from passing you on a busy expressway, one of the least pleasant sights you may encounter during your lifetime.

Here is another word of warning. Inside the whangdoodle on the trailer tongue are a pair of glimps that are supposed to clutch on to the doohickey. The glimps resemble little steel jaws, as I tend to think of them. Sometimes the jaws jam up when they come into contact with the doohickey. Here is the warning: Do not stick your finger up between the whang-doodle and the doohickey in an effort to unjam the jaws. Otherwise, you can forget about any future career as a brain surgeon. And don't get the idea that I am a brain surgeon. If I were a brain surgeon, I could hire somebody else to hook up my trailer lights.

Silent but Deadly

Although I've always made an effort to avoid gross and insensitive topics in these discourses, I believe the time has come for me to take a serious look at dog flatulence. When I say "look" I don't mean that, except in extreme cases, you can actually *see* dog flatulence, but only that it deserves some study, particularly by those of us who share with bird dogs the enclosed cab of a vehicle.

First of all, when these unfortunate occurrences take place, you should not yell at the dog. It will do no good and may only make matters worse. The dog, too, is suffering, as is perhaps obvious when he shoots you that pained little grin. There's no point in making him feel worse than he already does.

The reason this crude topic has come to mind is that the other day I was passed on the highway by some friends of mine returning from a pheasant hunt and driving well over the speed limit. Not only did the dogs have their heads hanging out the vehicle's windows, so did the hunters. It was a practice I myself have engaged in from time to time while hunting with my dog,

Clem the Recalcitrant. Nevertheless, I think it an extremely unsafe procedure, and decided that I should write a piece in which I offer a remedy for this unfortunate malady, one that contributes so much to the downside of bird hunting.

After contemplating the matter for several hours, however, and even with Clem under my desk doing his best to keep my mind on the topic, I was unable to come up with a remedy. So my only useful advice is, Live with it! My contemplation, nevertheless, reminded me of a social disaster perpetrated by my miserable old dog Strange, whom I more or less owned during my teenage years. I will relate that catastrophe here instead.

My mother had named the dog Stranger in the hope, as she later claimed, that he was just passing through. He wasn't. He stayed on for a dozen years, biting the hands that fed him, those hands usually belonging to my grandmother. He was the kind of dog that, had he been human, would probably have made his living as a loan shark working out of the trunk of his car. A relatively small dog of mixed breed, and possibly of mixed species, he possessed a high degree of intelligence which, as far as anyone ever noticed anyway, he never put to the service of the family that had taken him in. Indeed, had our house caught fire, the arson investigators might have come up with the standard photo of the crowd of spectators, one of whom might be the arsonist himself. In the front row, I'm quite sure, would have been a little brown-and-white dog, a look of bemusement on his face and possibly a can of kerosene next to him. I don't mean to imply that Strange, as his name was eventually and more appropriately shortened to, was the worst dog in the world, but if you were to reverse the Boy Scout motto you would pretty much define his character: untrustworthy, disloyal, unhelpful, etc.

The event in question began shortly after my family had stuffed itself with the typical Thanksgiving dinner. I lay suffering on the couch, in deep remorse over my recent gluttony and regretting that I had asked my former girlfriend, Olga Bonemarrow, to go to a movie with me that evening. I couldn't even consider breaking the date, because it was my first one since Olga had broken up with me the last time. She severed our relationship, as she had explained, because she thought we should each start dating other people and also because I was insensitive, inattentive, inane, ignorant, and gross.

I vaguely heard my grandmother call to my mother, "What do you want me to do with all this leftover turkey gravy?" Mom replied, "Whatever." I then heard Gram open the door to the utility room, where Strange resided during cold weather. If it occurred to me that it might be a very bad idea to feed turkey gravy to a dog, I don't recall, maybe because I could foresee no consequence for me.

The next parameter of the disaster was a mountain car my friend Retch Sweeney and I had bought together to use on our camping trips. The car had come without a backseat, as well as without brakes, headlights, taillights, spare tire, various windows, tailpipe, muffler, front fenders, and assorted other accessories. The partition between the backseat and the trunk had either rusted out or been cut out by us; I can't recall which. It was inside this convenient space that we stored all our camping gear—sleeping bags, tarps, etc.—and in which we sometimes slept, out of concern for the elements, primarily bears, wolves, cougars, and snakes. We named the car Miss Peabody, in honor of our favorite high school English teacher.

Now, you must try to visualize this next part, as I myself had to do in reconstructing the scene of the crime. Strange is slurping up—*"yowp gobble glub urp slurp choke glub"*—his massive serving of turkey gravy, augmented with other Thanksgiving edibles. Finished, he is booted out into the cold by Gram. Shortly thereafter, he begins to inflate. His skin grows taut over his body, which expands until it gradually envelops his legs up to his paws. Only half of his tail protrudes. He takes on the appearance of a small hairy zeppelin. Slowly, he rises off the ground. Using his paws as flippers and the tip of his tail as a rudder, he floats around the house until he arrives at Miss Peabody, the mountain car. He enters through an open window. Then he snuggles down under the camping gear and, presumably, goes to sleep. He is a ticking time bomb.

It was about this time that I said to my mother, "Well, it's almost time to pick up Olga. I'd better go crank Miss Peabody."

"I really hate that," Mom said.

"Yeah, me, too," I agreed. "The last time I tried to crank her, she kicked back and nearly broke my arm."

"Get out of here," Mom said.

I finally got the snow scraped off Miss Peabody, started her up, and drove over to the Bonemarrows. Olga came out of the house wearing a coat with a fur collar and a matching fur hat, and she was truly a vision of loveliness, her thick blond hair cascading down over her shoulders and her blue eyes sparkling in the crisp cold air. My heart leaped at the sight of her. It was hard to imagine that this was the same girl who a few brief years earlier threw me down, grabbed my ears, and beat my head up and down on the ground. She was carrying a flat, open box of pastries.

"What's that for?" I asked hopefully.

"Oh," she said, in her honeysuckle voice, "they're some pastries Mother and I made for the church bake sale tomorrow. Mind if we drop them off on the way to the movie?"

"Not at all. That is just so nice of you and your mom, helping the poor," I replied sensitively.

We headed off toward the church.

"You look very nice this evening," I said attentively.

"Thank you," she replied.

"You have a nice Thanksgiving?" I asked, trying to avoid the inane.

"Very nice," she said. "And you?"

"Oh, yes, indeed. Very nice."

We were about halfway to the church when Strange, suddenly, silently, sinisterly, deflated.

Later, trying to reconstruct the event, I thought I might have heard a faint *whooosh*, but by then I'd suffered so much brain damage I couldn't be sure. Olga and I were instantly engulfed by a plume of fume so powerful it fogged my glasses and sent tears streaming down my face. If Miss Peabody had had a speed faster than seven miles an hour, I might have driven off the road. (On the plus side, though, the fume ate most of the rust off the dashboard.) I couldn't believe this was happening.

Naturally, as far as I was at the moment aware, there could be only one suspect for this atmospheric atrocity.

My eyes streaming tears, I glanced at the suspect. Her eyes bored into me like a matched pair of stilettos. Her face glowed a fiery red. *She is obviously embarrassed,* I thought. And rightfully so! I was about to blurt out a gross comment, when I suddenly caught myself. No point in risking another breakup, even though at the moment Olga's appeal had somewhat diminished for me. I tried frantically to come up with something sensitive to say, something attentive, something that wasn't gross. The box of pastries on her lap drew my attention. There was a particularly large cherry tart sitting on top. I leaned over and nodded at it, pretending I'd noticed absolutely nothing of an olfactory nature.

"You do that big one?" I choked out.

Driving home alone shortly thereafter, or not quite alone, because the true villain had emerged by then to take as much credit for the ruckus as he could, I was pulled over by Sheriff

Bonemarrow, who just happened to be Olga's father. He hated Miss Peabody, the car, and from time to time had actually threatened Retch and me with bodily harm if he caught us driving it on the highway again. Fortunately, that night I was on a back road. The sheriff took off his hat and used it to fan his way through the black cloud of exhaust.

"What do you burn in this thing?" he growled. "Wet leaves?" It was his standard line. He glanced around the inside of Miss Peabody. "Where's Olga? I thought you and Olga were going to a movie tonight."

"Naw, Olga broke up with me again."

"What this time?"

"The usual. Inattentive, insensitive, inane, and gross. Particularly gross."

"Women!" he said.

"Yeah," I said. "Women."

"One other thing, Patrick. What's that red stuff all over your face? Better not be lipstick!"

"Cherry tart," I said. "It's cherry tart. What happened was, Olga grabbed the tart—"

The sheriff held up his hand. "Stop, I don't want to know. One more thing, though."

"What's that?" I said.

"Why's your dog riding on the roof of the car? He looks half froze."

"Turkey gravy," I said. "Gram fed him turkey gravy."

"Turkey gravy! Fed a dog turkey gravy in a populated area! I think that's a felony! I should go arrest her!"

"I wish you would," I said.

Excuses Excuses

Ms. Camille Rankin, Managing Editor
OUTDOOR LIFE Magazine
Two Park Avenue
New York , NY 10016

My dear Camille,

At this very minute you're probably saying to yourself, "Why haven't I received this month's column from that lovable old rascal Pat? I hope he isn't going to come up with another excuse about how his dog ate his humor column and then went around for two days cracking jokes."

Listen, Camille, sweetheart, I know you found out about the dog, namely that I don't have one. That's behind us, okay? There's no reason to keep dwelling on a nonexistent dog. There are things much more important in life, such as boats. As you know, I actually do have a boat—wife, children, house, job, and boat, the full catastrophe. If I didn't have wife, children, house, and job, I'd probably have almost enough time to take care of the boat.

So what I am getting at here is that my boat ate the column. Well, actually, it wasn't the boat that ate it but possibly my friend Fenton Quagmire. But the boat was an accessory to the crime. Here is exactly what happened, every word a virtual paragon of Truth. (Forget about the stupid dog!)

Once again I had underestimated Fenton Quagmire's deficiencies—physical, mental, and hygienic—for assisting me with even the simplest chore, in this instance the launching of my boat at Echo Bay Resort on Lake Roosevelt, where I had rented a slip for the summer.

The original problem arose when the Corps of Engineers got to fooling around with the lake level and dropped it—no one knows how—about 50 feet down into the canyon, leaving the resort's launch ramp high and dry. This meant that I would have to launch my boat at Twilight Bay, ten miles up the lake. Therefore I'd need someone for the simple task of driving either the truck and trailer or the boat back to Echo Bay.

"No, no, not in a thousand years!" roared Quagmire, hamming it up as usual. "Your disasters make a practice of parading themselves as simple chores! The last ten times I've helped you with something it has turned into a disaster!" (I make an innocent little request and Quagmire responds by doing King Lear!)

"I know," I said. "But I'm willing to overlook that.

I'm quite confident that if you'll keep your mind on what you're doing we will avoid any such unhappy events on this occasion."

Quagmire at last relented and agreed to help with the launching. As we towed the boat out to the resort, I once again emphasized to him that he must pay absolute attention to what he was doing, because he has this tendency to allow any little thing to distract him from the task at hand. I was therefore not at all surprised when, even as I spoke, I heard him mutter something about being late for a dinner he was supposed to attend that evening. As I understood it, he was to receive a golf trophy of some sort.

"Now, that's exactly what I've been warning you against, Fenton," I scolded. "Why on earth would you be thinking about food and golf this evening when it's not yet even noon and we're on our way to launch a boat?"

"Because you just drove past the turnoff to Twilight Bay, that's why!"

"Very good, Fenton," I said. "I was checking to see if you were paying attention. And believe me, it's well worth the extra hour it will take us to get back to the turnoff. You have increased my confidence in you no end."

We arrived at Twilight Bay without my having further need to test Quagmire's concentration and soon had the boat launched. Quagmire hopped in the boat, still muttering. Let me say at this point that his task was no more complicated than to drive the boat back to Echo Bay Resort, tie it up in the slip, and then meet me in the parking lot for the drive home. I had decided it was best if Quagmire drove the boat back, rather than the truck and trailer, because the tangle of roads could be quite confusing for a person unfamiliar with them and the more so for a person prone to daydreaming, as I'm quite certain Fenton is. If distracted even for a moment, he could be crossing the Canadian border before he knew it.

"Okay, Fenton," I explained. "All you have to do is navigate down the lake for approximately ten miles. You will see Echo Bay Marina on your left. If you don't see it on your left, you might check your right. It is there someplace. You can't miss it."

"That's good to know," Fenton replied, being careful to conceal his relief.

"Yes," I said. "It's quite simple. All you have to do is stay in the lake and you have a straight shot at Echo Bay. I, on the other hand, have to wend my way through numerous hairpin turns, over two mountains, and among numerous divergent roads. You will no doubt reach the resort a good twenty minutes ahead of me. So don't worry about me if I'm a few minutes late."

Quagmire responded with a maniacal laugh, when, as it turned out, he should have had his mind on the business at hand. I gave the boat a hard shove off. The current of Twilight Creek caught the craft and swept it out into the lake. It was only at that point that Fenton gave me a wave. Even though I was thoroughly irritated with him and his cavalier manner, I waved back. Quagmire continued to wave until he was swept around the first bend and out of sight. He was yelling, too, although I found him to be quite inaudible. Maybe my wife is right that I should get my hearing checked. Undoubtedly, he was probably still trying to remind me about his dinner and trophy. The guy simply won't quit.

Strangely, I ran into a bit of a traffic jam on my way back to the border and was delayed for well over an hour. It wasn't a total loss, though, because it had been years since I had seen any Canadian Mounties in their dress uniforms. Of all uniforms, I think the Mounties' are the most spectacular. Reacting quickly to what might have been a difficult situation, I whipped a quick U-turn and headed back down the highway toward Echo Bay. Fenton, if he hadn't drifted off into some ridiculous daydream, would have arrived sometime earlier.

When I got back to Echo Bay, I was not entirely surprised to find no boat and no Fenton! How could I even guess where he might have ended up? I sat there in the truck twiddling my thumbs and staring down at the empty slip and chastising myself for putting my boat in Quagmire's care. That's when I realized what had happened. Fenton had forgotten to ask me for the key to the boat's ignition! It was just the sort of thing I had come to expect from him. The man simply lacked even the feeblest powers of observation. Well, I had no one to blame but Quagmire. I could scarcely believe I had once again trusted him to carry out an important but simple task. Well, he would have used the little trolling motor to get him back to the dock. It might have taken him a while, because there is quite a bit of current along that side of the lake, but an easy enough job for the 7-horse, if Fenton had thought to fill its gas tank. It was just like him to overlook a detail like that, though.

I immediately sped the ten miles back to Twilight Bay, which for some reason took an hour and twenty minutes, one of those strange lapses in time that make you think there might really be something to the stories about alien abductions, although I felt none of the physical discomfort you hear reported by the various abductees. And thank goodness for that!

I found Fenton and the boat back at the dock at Twilight Bay Resort. Quagmire was sitting on a box whittling something. He looked tired, but I thought this might not be the time to lecture him on physical fitness.

"How long before you remembered the key?" I asked, pleasantly enough. Quagmire's eyes rolled back in his head and appeared to be stuck there. I thought for a moment he might be suffering a seizure of some kind. Fortunately, he recovered before I could pry his mouth far enough open to grab his tongue and keep him from swallowing it.

"The KEY!" he roared. "Oh, yes, that, too! But how about the DRAIN PLUG?"

"You forgot the drain plug, too?" I gasped. "Well, you have certainly outdone yourself this time, Fenton. By the way, I have a drain plug in the glove compartment of the truck. Remember, Fenton, always check the glove box of the truck before you set out in the boat. It's one of the first rules of safe boating, although seldom mentioned in the little

Coast Guard pamphlets. So you don't have to finish whittling another drain plug."

"It's not a drain plug," Quagmire growled. "It's a doll of you."

"How thoughtful of you," I replied, not a little touched by emotion. "I'll hang it on my rearview mirror."

Quagmire gave me one of his maniacal smiles. "I'll hang it myself," he said.

"So let's get this affair ended," I said. "This time you drive the truck to Echo Bay and I'll drive the boat." That's when the trouble started, of course. As I say, you simply cannot depend upon Quagmire to carry out a simple task like helping you launch a boat without him somehow messing up the whole business. Nevertheless, we eventually met up again at the Echo Bay marina.

But Fenton wasn't done with me yet. We had no more started home than he told me to stop at a park so he could use the restroom.

"Boy, if it's not one thing it's another with you, Quagmire," I told him.

He stomped over and jerked open the door marked MEN. Then he jerked open the door marked WOMEN. He turned around and shouted back at me, "Just as I suspected! They're all out of toilet tissue!"

"Tough luck," I said. "Come on, let's go!"

"Nope, I always plan ahead for emergencies like this. What I do is—"

"Spare me the details!" I yelled.

Now, here's the unusual thing, Camille.

Despite all of Quagmire's raving and fooling around, we made it back to town in plenty of time for him to attend his dinner and get his award. The post office was still open, too, so that I could get my column mailed off to you.

But the manuscript was gone! Missing! Vanished without a trace! And I'd had it right here on the front seat between me and Quagmire all day. You don't suppose a dog could have come along and eaten it, do you?

Yours truly,
Pat

Splitting Infinitives

I was twelve years old, sitting in Mr. Arthur B. Snopes's English class at Delmore Blight Junior High. It was September. I still had more than eight months of Mr. Snopes's English class. Already I knew I would not be able to stand it.

Mr. Snopes did not actually teach English. He taught grammar. He didn't exactly teach grammar. You may find this hard to believe, but what he did, he had this little auger with which he bored a hole in the head of each pupil. He then took a small funnel, stuck it in the hole, and poured in grammar. Naturally, we students didn't ever use any of the grammar, because it was so precious, had been obtained with such misery, such excruciating boredom, that we couldn't stand to spend a bit of it.

Mr. Snopes was what I now call an anti–role model. In other words, you did not want to be like Mr. Snopes when you grew up. He was short, stocky, bald, and, despite being a teacher, possessed the ruddy complexion of an outdoorsman. Through the school-yard grapevine I had heard that Mr.

Snopes lived on a farm several miles from town. Every morning he would get up at four, milk the cows, slop the hogs, and
feed the chickens. Then he would go into the house and put
on his blue wool pants, his white shirt, a tie, and his rusty-
brown cardigan sweater, which may have been made out of
iron, because it never seemed to wear out. Then he would pick
up the student papers he had spent the night correcting, the
lard pail with his lunch in it, and his head auger and funnel,
and drive to school.

The last ten or fifteen minutes of each class period, Mr.
Snopes would give us some grammatical problem to solve.
While we slaved away at our desks, he would hunch down
over a batch of papers, a green eyeshade over his eyes. At the
end of class we would get back the problems we had worked on
the previous day, but there would be so many red marks and
notes on them that they were practically useless.

As I said, it was only September and already I knew I would
not be able to stand another eight months of Mr. Snopes and
his grammar. So I would wait until the teacher turned to the
chalkboard and began to diagram a sentence or perform one
of his other fiendish tortures, and then I would slip out the
second-story window, rush down the fire escape, cross the play-
ground, and head for Greenhorn Mountain.

The mountain could easily be seen from Mr. Snopes's class-
room. From a distance it appeared easy to climb, but I knew
from experience that it in fact offered a very difficult ascent,
at least from the east side. The mountain seemingly had been
constructed out of a series of loaves, each one higher than the
previous one, and with a deep drop between them. This would
give the climber the mistaken impression that he was nearing
the top of the mountain when in fact he would be nearing only
the top of a loaf. Then he would have to descend some distance, cross a more or less level area, and start up the next loaf.

Although a nuisance for a mountain climber, the area be-tween the loaves was perfect for an escapee from an English class. It offered protection from the wind and concealment from Mr. Snopes.

On particularly bad days of grammar, by which I mean all of them, I would slip off to the mountain and build a wickiup. I'm not sure how I knew about wickiups at that young age, but many years later, while wandering around the wilds of Montana, I occasionally came across the weathered remains of a wickiup that Indians had built as a temporary shelter during a much earlier time. (Perhaps they, too, had grammar classes, but I hate to think so.) My wickiup was every bit as good as the Indians'. To build a wickiup, I should point out, you simply lean logs and sticks and whatever else you can find around a tree until you have an enclosed shelter. It's nifty. You can even build a fire in it, if you're freezing to death, or totally wacko.

Once I had my wickiup built, which took but a couple of minutes, I would shoot a deer and maybe an elk, tan the skin, and make myself some clothes. I would salt the venison and then smoke strips of it over a willow fire, preserving enough to last me through the winter. It was hard work, but nothing like sitting through Mr. Snopes's grammar class.

Occasionally, I would slip down to Little Sand Creek, which wound around the base of the mountain. The creek fur-nished the town of Blight City with its water supply. For that reason, fishing there was off-limits but extremely good, and I would soon have a nice mess of fish, which I would also smoke and preserve for the winter. If the reader is put off by this bit of criminality, or perhaps quenches his thirst from the water sup-ply of Blight City, he should remember that I was already on the lam from Delmore Blight Junior High. One more violation meant nothing to me.

I did not spend nights in the wickiup. Still working on sleeping out alone in the dark, I used the shelter only during the day, actually only for about fifty minutes a day, or roughly the same time span as Mr. Snopes's class.

Every day I would in this manner escape from the teacher's relentless attack with dangling participles, split infinitives, and other abominations. They should not allow such things in schools. (Apparently, these days, they don't. And people actually complain that education isn't what it used to be!) It was only Greenhorn Mountain that saved me, from that September all the way through till the following May, a few weeks before the end of school. Perhaps that is why, even now, I think of mountains as places of escape.

One day during grammar class, I was seated in front of my wickiup toasting a marshmallow over a fire, in typical mountain-man fashion, when the urge came upon me to climb to the top of the next loaf. It took me but seconds, such was my fine physical condition from all the time I had spent on the mountain. Upon coming over the top of the loaf, however, I was startled to see down in the next gap another wickiup. A person was seated in front of it, toasting a marshmallow over a fire. Naturally, I was disappointed that some other malcontent should have discovered my means of escape. I approached cautiously, only to be startled out of my wits when the individual leaped up and shouted at me.

"Ha, Patrick!" cried Mr. Snopes. "I suppose you think you are the only person who has a need to escape! Why do you think I wear that green eyeshade, hunh?"

Many years later I was dozing in a freshman composition course at college, when the young professor asked, "Can anyone here tell me the three verbals?"

I raised my hand.

"Yes?" he said.

"Infinitives, gerunds, and participles," I said.

"Correct," the professor said, obviously surprised and disappointed.

Now, where did that come from? I asked myself, scratching the small round spot on the back of my head.

Don't Annoy My
Inner Frontiersman

A couple of years ago I was up in the wilds of Alaska, look-ing around for my guide. When you're in the wilds of Alaska—think grizzly—it's a good idea not to get too far from your guide.

I finally found him looking into the palm of his hand. It seemed likely he was studying a twig with moss on it to figure out which way was north. It used to be that guides were always interested in the direction of north. I don't know why. The only direction I was ever seriously interested in was the way back to camp. So I asked Rolf, my guide, what he was doing, hoping for some sort of exotic lore that I might someday put to use.

"Checking my messages," he said.

"Checking your messages?" I said. Up until then I hadn't realized he was some sort of mystic. Maybe Nature herself was providing him with important clues as to our whereabouts. "You doing that with a leaf or something?" I said.

He frowned. "No, a BlackBerry."

"Wow!" I said. "A blackberry. That's wonderful. Anything of particular interest?"

"Naw, just something from my girlfriend."

Well, I was dumbfounded. Then he held up a little instrument. "This," he said, "is a BlackBerry!"

Naturally, I was crestfallen. Or, rather, my Inner Frontiersman was. In fact, my Inner Frontiersman was severely disappointed. I go to all the time and expense to take my Inner Frontiersman to the wilderness of Alaska, and what happens? My guide is picking up messages from his girlfriend! What is the world coming to? Or rather, where is it going?

Not long before I was in the wilds of Alaska, I was in the wilds of British Columbia. One day my friend Jim Zumbo called the *Outdoor Life* office in New York. On his cell phone! Here we have grizzly bears and black bears and wolves and moose running all over the place, and Zumbo is talking on the phone to New York. He probably could hear police car and fire engine sirens in the background. Is my Inner Frontiersman not safe anywhere from technology?

I started to complain about Zumbo to one of the other outdoor writers on the expedition, and he said, "I'm sorry, but I can't talk now. I have to file a story to my magazine." He pulled out a laptop computer and began typing. We're out in the wilds of Canada and he's still working as if he is down the hall at the office! My Inner Frontiersman couldn't believe it.

I should have suspected something like this would happen someday, but it all came on so fast, my Inner Frontiersman can't adjust. Part of the problem is that I was born too long ago. My first fishing rod, for example, was actually a slender tamarack pole about twelve feet long. It had a length of line the same length as the pole. The line was tied to the tip of the pole and you could fasten the hook into the end of the butt if you so wished. The line contained a sinker about the size of a cowbell, and down from the sinker a ways was the hook. You baited the hook with a worm. The entire contraption cost about three cents. But it caught fish. The landing technique consisted of flipping the pole straight up and sending the fish over your head. Sometimes the fish came off in mid-flip and you had to hunt for it in the brush or sometimes up in a tree. That was part of the fun. It was real fishing. And you kept everything you caught, because that's what you did with fish back then.

By contrast, nowadays, my rich friend Fenton Quagmire has a thirty-thousand-dollar fishing boat. He has numerous other boats, but the cheap thirty-thousand-dollar one is what he uses for regular everyday fishing. It is equipped with every technological gadget known to man. It saves Quagmire the trouble of actually going fishing. He can send the boat out by itself. The craft is practically human. He can even program it to forget the drain plug, just to provide some realistic excitement. Quagmire sits at home and watches his boat fish on a couple of television screens. "Wow, that's a nice one!" he shouts. The boat even tells lies. Once it was only a block away but transmitting phony pictures. Quagmire thought it was some of the best fishing he'd ever had. Okay, I'm exaggerating. Actually the boat cost a lot more than thirty thousand dollars.

One of my favorite mottoes is, Never think too hard about anything you enjoy doing. I made that up myself, but it works for me. Take camping, for instance. Why on earth do you leave a nice comfortable home to go out and cook over a campfire, get smoke in your eyes from the fire, shooting pains in your back from sleeping on the ground, sopping wet from the rain that usually accompanies any camping trip, and so on? You do it because your Inner Frontiersman enjoys doing it. Just don't think about it too much.

Every so often one of our local criminals will flee into the mountains, leaving behind a message that he is going to hunt and fish for his food and otherwise live off the land and be free to do as he pleases. A week later, dressed in camos and with burned cork all over his face, he is arrested at a McDonald's. He is thin and shaky and wolfing down two Big Macs and a couple of shakes. Mother Nature is brutal out there in the mountains. I want to tell the criminal, "Living wild and free is a fantasy, dumbo! Don't mess with turning it into reality. Just exercise your Inner Frontiersman from time to time."

Yes, it's all fantasy, at least my fantasy, and that of my Inner Frontiersman. I don't like folks irritating my Inner Frontiersman, such as guides checking messages on their BlackBerries. As with many other Americans, I am, at heart, a frontiersman—a somewhat overweight and flabby frontiersman, but a frontiersman nevertheless. I think it's important to know how to fish and to catch fish, even though I can get all the fish I want at a supermarket and a whole lot cheaper. But going to the supermarket doesn't satisfy my Inner Frontiersman. I like coming home with the five trout our local law allows me to keep and for me to be able to tell my wife, Bun, "Look, we eat for another week!" Bun's response often causes my Inner Frontiersman severe depression, but that's not the point.

Don't get me started on fly-fishing. True, most of my friends are fly-fishermen, and I don't like to deflate their own particular illusions. But fly-fishing has just about ruined fishing for me. It simply isn't satisfying to my Inner Frontiersman. Somehow, in recent years, fly-fishermen turned the act of fishing into an art form. Now it's all about the grace quotient in their loop. They think of themselves as Picassos in waders. The fish themselves are sort of bystanders. *What's this guy doing?* they ask themselves. *Does he think we can't tell that bit of fuzz from a fly? Well, maybe we should humor him and take a bite. He'll just release us anyway. Hey, it'll be fun!*

Nobody has yet ruined hunting for my Inner Frontiersman. You bring home a deer or elk or moose, that's serious provisions for the winter. Sometimes, though, our electricity goes off for a day or so. My Inner Frontiersman starts to panic about the temperature in the freezer. I suspect the feeling is akin to that of the frontiersman a few centuries ago, hearing a strange cry drift through the night. My Inner Frontiersman, of course, responds in the same way to danger. He thinks, *What will I do if the electricity doesn't come back on? Not only am I faced with the threat of my air conditioner failing to work, but my cache of venison is in danger of spoiling!*

Fortunately, there's a McDonald's a few blocks away, so I won't starve. On the other hand, my Inner Frontiersman tends to choke up when ordering two Big Macs and a side of fries.

Camping Out with Lewis & Clark

Many years ago I bought a three-volume set of the journals of Lewis and Clark. It took me four years to read them, one year more than the expedition itself. The experience was harrowing. Many times I thought I would perish along the way, leaving my bleached bones to be discovered years later in my tattered old slide rocker.

I don't know how many times I found myself lost and alone in volume I, particularly between St. Louis and the Mandan village. Indeed, when Lewis and Clark and their men reached the village, I was more than happy to winter over there with them. I became so transfixed by studying the Mandans' method of making beads, the expedition slipped away without my knowing, and I didn't catch up with them again until the following spring, when Mount St. Helens erupted and I was trapped inside the house by a six-inch blanket of volcanic ash spread across the Pacific Northwest. Anyone trapped indoors with four kids, a dog, two cats, and a gerbil, not to mention a spouse displaying homicidal tendencies, could not help but look upon the so-called travails of the Lewis and Clark expedition as minor irritations.

As a result of my perusing the journals so studiously, I have come up with a number of questions and observations that historians may wish to ponder. Then again, maybe not.

For example, exactly how did President Jefferson propose to Meriwether Lewis that he take an expedition from one side of the American continent to the other and then back again?

Jefferson: "Good day to you, Meriwether. I called you over to see how you feel about camping out."

Lewis: "Oh, I enjoy it very much, sir. During my vacation last summer, I camped out for nearly a week. Some of the fellows and I gathered around the campfire every evening and sang and told ghost stories and roasted marshmallows. Yes, indeed, I do enjoy camping out."

Jefferson: "Very good, Meriwether, very good! Then I know you will be pleased to undertake the little jaunt I have in mind."

Although my memory is a bit foggy on this point, I believe that it was President Jefferson himself who recommended Dr. Benjamin Rush to Lewis. Whether he did this in jest is unclear. The fact that Dr. Rush was a member of the American Philosophical Society, however, should have been a clue. There is no mention of his having belonged to the American Medical Association, which is another clue.

Dr. Rush provided Lewis with a sizable quantity of Rush's Pills, although it seems likely that even one pill would have been excessive. According to historian Stephen E. Ambrose in his excellent history of the expedition, *Undaunted Courage*, Rush's Pills were generally referred to by the men on the expedition as "Thunderclappers," although no particular reason is given. Again, according to Ambrose, the pills were "composed of calomel, a mixture of six parts mercury to one part chlorine, and jalap. Each drug was a purgative of explosive power; the combination was awesome." As a historian, Ambrose does not use the word *awesome* casually.

Rush's Pills proved extraordinarily helpful to Lewis and Clark in keeping the expedition members in excellent health. Whenever a man came to Lewis complaining about an illness, injury, or fatigue, Meriwether would administer up to three pills. After a short while, complaints dwindled to the occasional moan or cough, quickly attributed by the source to "goofing around."

The journals suggest that the pills had enormous restorative powers. I don't recall any specific instances, but let us suppose that during the expedition, a man by the name of Otis Spikofski got separated from the main party and was lost for three days. When found, he appeared to be dead. Considering this an extreme case, Lewis administered a dose of six pills. Spikofski instantly revived and propelled the expedition's craft ten miles upstream all by himself. The rest of the expeditionary force, rather than accompany Spikofski on the craft, chose instead to slog ten miles through a swamp. No reason is given for this display of churlishness by the men.

Most of the journals were written by Lewis, which may explain why Captain Clark is seldom mentioned. I myself often receive criticism from persons who accompany me on camping trips because they are seldom mentioned in my articles. "You are in every sentence practically, and we weren't even mentioned once. Besides, the facts are all wrong." That is the way the complaint is commonly phrased. I respond, "If you want to be mentioned, write your own story. And don't bother me anymore about facts." I am sure Lewis responded in similar fashion to any complaints from Clark. It is one of the main rewards of writing a journal.

Lewis was a master of understatement. A typical journal

entry might go something like this: "Woke up at dawn. Fed the men cold gruel. It was raining and couldn't get fire started. A bear broke into camp and dragged off the man Spikofski. The expedition traveled upriver 15 miles. Saw a large herd of buffalo this evening."

A few days later, Lewis might write something like this: "Fed the men cold gruel this morning. Still no complaints. The bear dragged Spikofski back into camp during the night. He appeared to have been scarcely gnawed. As I approached his prostrate form with a handful of Rush's Pills, he leaped up and did the work of five men before we even broke camp. Saw a bald eagle about noon."

In my own wilderness travels, I have often crossed the Lewis and Clark trail, and I find much of the country not too different today from how it was described two hundred years ago. For example, when the expedition crossed what is now Idaho the men saw absolutely no game at all and were forced to shoot and eat their horses and dogs. Let me say that I have hunted that same area of Idaho and have seen absolutely no game at all, either. I didn't have any horses or dogs to eat as a means of sating my hunger, but I should mention that my companions didn't get much sleep. Fortunately, we were soon found by Clearwater Search and Rescue.

The leader of the patrol said, "I thought there were three men on your expedition."

"No," I said. "Only two."

Lewis seems generally of the opinion that the indigenous peoples he meets along his route are pleased to see a group of armed white men traveling through their territory. For example, he calmly writes in the entry for March 13, 1804: "We had a fine day and a southwest wind. Mr. M'Kenzie came to see us, as did also many Indians, who are so anxious for battle-axes that our smiths have not a moment of leisure. . . ." But perhaps I'm the only reader who found that entry amusing.

I do hope within the next couple of years to follow the Lewis and Clark trail from Independence to the Pacific Ocean at Seaside, Oregon. I told my wife, Bun, that she and I would live off the land.

She said, "I'm not going unless we eat in restaurants."

"That's what I mean," I said.

I am sure our journey will be nowhere near as rigorous as the Lewis and Clark expedition, unless, of course, the price of gas stays as high as it is right now. (And Meriwether thinks his men had it tough! Ha!) Still, I will take along my three-volume set of the journals, and will read myself to sleep with the entry for each correlative day of the journey:

"May 29th.—We set sail at four o'clock [P.M.] and at four miles distance camped on the south side above a small creek, called Deer Creek and . . ." ZZZZZZ . . .

Strange Meets His Match

Someone told me recently that a fairly exact correlation exists between a diminishing intelligence quotient and the ownership of dogs. If I understand it correctly, the IQ drops five points for every dog acquired over the years. That would put my present IQ at about 40. A few more dogs and I won't have any IQ at all. I'll be down in the negative numbers. My wife, Bun, agrees with that assessment, and she is a lot better at math than I am, due largely, I suppose, to the number of dogs I've owned.

My present dog, Clem, is totally useless. He spends most of each day sleeping under my desk. Every time I hear the expression "That dog won't hunt," I think of Clem. I don't think he was designed for hunting, anyway, so I can't really blame him for that. What he was designed for I have no idea. He's pretty good at sleeping under my desk, so perhaps that is what his designer had in mind.

Besides sleeping under my desk, Clem's other great pleasure is riding with me out to the dump. I can't criticize him for that, because going to the dump is also one of my great pleasures. Discarding all that useless stuff somehow gives me a sense of accomplishment. Acquiring it years ago probably gave me a sense of accomplishment, too. Clem, of course, doesn't discard anything at the dump, or at least anything I've caught him at. I think his joy comes primarily from the cookie.

Some time ago, a new lady took over the pay shack at the dump, and she leaned out the little window and inquired, "Would the shaggy old snookums like a cookie?" This sort of thing happens to me quite often, so right away I said, "Sure." I have to tell you, that cookie was about the worst thing I've ever tasted. So as soon as we were out of sight of the pay shack, I gave the cookie to Clem. He loved it. Among his other deficiencies, Clem has no taste.

When we got home, I told Bun about the cookie incident. She responded by looking first at me and then at Clem and then back at me. She said, "Have you ever heard the theory that after a while dogs and their owners start to look like each other?"

I don't know where Bun picks up this kind of nonsense, but Clem seemed almost as offended as I was.

I am not a person who has ever shopped for dogs. All my life I have simply acquired them. They show up at my house and decide to stay on until they expire. Maybe there is some kind of marker on my front gate, put there many years ago by a hobo dog. The marker more or less means, "This guy is a sucker for stray dogs." It's also staining my gate post.

I got my first dog when I was five or six. For some unknown reason, he was called Happy. I would play little practical jokes on Happy, and he would bite me. That was pretty much our relationship. Even now, when my hands get tan in the summer, you can see the little white bite marks on my fingers. At least I think that's where the marks came from.

After Happy, I had one or two inconsequential dogs, and then Strange arrived. In appearance, Strange seemed at first to be your simple little brown-and-white dog. Upon closer inspection, however, you would notice that he had a scraggly mustache that drooped down on both sides of his mouth. His nose was rather prominent for a dog, and on each side of it were little bulging eyes about the size of double-ought buckshot, and just as hard, too.

New friends of mine from school would occasionally drop by. "Geez," they would say, "is that your dog?"

I would usually admit that he was, although sometimes I might lie and say, "Naw, I think he's just passing through."

In the middle of Strange's sojourn with us, which, as my grandmother claimed, lasted about forever, I acquired my one and only registered bird dog, a beautiful Irish setter. His name was Butch Garrion III. He actually belonged to the local Catholic priest, Father O'Toole. The arrangement was that we would house and feed the dog, and Father O'Toole would come out to the farm and use him during pheasant season. I, for one, approved of the arrangement, because otherwise Father O'Toole would use me for a bird dog. "Here, boy! Here, boy! C'mon, boy," he'd call out. "See what you can flush out of that thorn thicket. Be quick about it now!" So I was glad to be replaced by Butch. I don't know how good of a bird dog he was, because Father O'Toole never got any pheasants. I suppose somebody should have told him we hadn't seen a pheasant on the farm in years.

The one nice thing about Butch was that he was beautiful. Dumb as stone, but beautiful. Whenever a friend stopped by and asked, "Is that your dog?" I'd say, "Yeah. He's registered."

"Who's the other one?"

"Don't know. He's just passing through."

One summer my mother decided we would drive down to

Lewiston, Idaho, and pick fruit. Butch was sent back to his owner, but that left Strange.

"What about Strange?" I asked my mother.

"I've arranged with Rancid Crabtree for Strange to stay with him."

"Rancid!" I exclaimed. "If Strange acts up, Rancid is liable to shoot him!"

"What's your point?" Mom said.

On the day we were to leave, I took Strange over to Rancid's shack, which he had built up against Greenhorn Mountain. He didn't have a dog of his own, which I thought a little suspicious. Everybody in our part of the country owned at least one dog. Back then, I didn't realize that not owning a dog was a sign of intelligence. Rancid's other sign of intelligence was that he had never worked at a job in his entire life. What little money he needed for tobacco and whiskey he made by running a trapline. It was the kind of life I had planned for myself, but I somehow got distracted.

Rancid stared down at Strange. Strange stared back.

"That it?" Rancid said.

"Afraid so."

"You hongry, dog?" Rancid said. He turned and took a skillet of leftover gravy off his barrel stove. "It's grouse gravy," he said. "Best gravy in the world." Even though it was summer and a long time before grouse season, I didn't bother to ask how he had managed to come up with a grouse for his gravy.

He set the skillet on the floor in front of Strange. The dog gobbled up the gravy and then licked the skillet clean.

"Wouldja lookit thet?" Rancid said. "Shoot, now, Ah won't even hef to wash maw skillet, not thet Ah was plannin' to anyways!"

"He's got a lot of bad habits," I said. "Some of them are even crimes he could be arrested for."

"Tell me one of his crimes," Rancid said.

I told him.

"Shucks, Ah never even know'd thet was a crime! Glad you told me."

I left Strange with Rancid, not at all sure the dog would survive until we returned. We went off to Lewiston and picked fruit until I was about ready to expire. After days and maybe weeks of this torture, we returned home. Right away I walked over to Rancid's shack, to see if Strange had survived. Rancid was sitting on his front porch in a rocking chair. Strange was lying beside him, gnawing on the skull of some unfortunate animal. They both looked pleased with themselves. I thanked Rancid and then called Strange. Picking up the skull, he reluctantly followed me home, but afterward scarcely a day went by that he didn't go over and hang out with Rancid. They seemed to enjoy each other's company.

"Two peas in a pod," my mother described them.

And she was right. One day they were sitting together on the porch, and I noticed that they both had scraggly mustaches that drooped down past the corners of their mouths, and on each side of their prominent noses they had little bulging eyes about the size of double-ought buckshot, and just as hard, too.

"Uh-oh!"

(And Other Things Guides Shouldn't Say)

During lunch on a guided float trip recently, several of us client-anglers got into a contest that consisted of thinking up the worst things we might hear from guides. Following is a sample of guide remarks with a tendency to cause concern for clients.

The most common guide utterance, we agreed, was "Uh-oh!" To which the clients yell, "What? *What!*" The guide then replies, "Nothing." Knowing he has to be lying, you are consumed by worry for the rest of the trip. If you are fortunate, you never learn of the calamity you managed to escape.

One of my own experiences with a guide's "Uh-oh!" occurred on a drift-boat trip down a river in quest of steelhead. As we approached the takeout, our guide looked up and saw a small band of game wardens checking catches and licenses. "Uh-oh!" he said.

"What? *What!*" we hissed at him.

"Nothing," he said. "But listen, guys, let's just pretend that

51

I'm not actually guiding you, okay? We're just a bunch of friends out fishing together, okay?"

It should have been fairly easy to pretend that our guide wasn't a guide, because we hadn't had so much as a nibble all day. Despite my reputation, however, I become extremely upset at even the hint of illegality or irregularity. I am also a very poor actor, particularly when it might come to covering up said illegality. Not knowing what our guide's possible crime might consist of—certainly not catching more than our limit of steelhead—I assumed it must be something to do with his guiding license. Either he had allowed it to lapse or he never had one in the first place. As it happened, I knew several of the game wardens at the takeout, and during the backslapping and joyous cries at our surprise meeting, I glanced around for our "guide." Both he and his boat had vanished downstream toward the Pacific Ocean. I have not laid eyes on him since. Perhaps he drifted out to sea and rowed to Mexico.

Speaking of Mexico, I have had many superb guides there and caught many fish as a result of their excellent service. One time I took two of my daughters, aged twelve and sixteen at the time, on a guided fishing trip out from the little town of Barra de Navidad. (It was little back then.) Our guide was ancient and the boat maybe twice as ancient. At one point, the motor stopped and the old man began tinkering with it. Then he looked up at the rocks toward which we were drifting. I looked at the same rocks. Waves were crashing against them in an impressive manner. Then the old man uttered the Spanish equivalent of "Uh-oh!"

"What's he saying?" one of my daughters asked.

"Nothing," I said.

Then the guide spoke again, his eyes pleading with me. I managed to pick up the word *destornillador*, a word not that easy to pick up. I think he was asking if I happened to have a screwdriver on me. I didn't, which was odd, since I almost always carry a screwdriver.

I shook my head no in Spanish.

Fortunately, the old man managed to get the motor going while we were still a good nine inches away from the rocks. Despite that close call, our guide turned out to be a fishing genius as well as a great mechanic, even without a *destornillador*. Among our other nice catches that day was a large needlefish. You have to be a true fisherman to think of a needlefish as a nice catch. I used a portion of it as bait while casting off a beach that night. The needlefish was snapped up by a huge pargo, the Mexican equivalent, I believe, of a red snapper. I traded the fish to Rosario, the owner of a beachfront restaurant, for all the garlic-shrimp dinners we could eat. It was all very wonderful. Still, my memory of that little fishing excursion remains dominated by the guide's utterance of "Uh-oh!" It is a guide expression neither easily ignored nor easily forgotten.

Here are some other comments clients would prefer not to hear from guides:

"Anyone here bring a compass?"

"Does this tree [rock, mountain] look familiar to anyone?"

"Might be a good idea for us to pick a bunch of these berries."

"Just because your horse is named Brimstone don't mean nothing."

"Lucky for you, I just sharpened my jackknife. Now let me take a look at that sliver [hook, leg, arm, finger, eye]."

"I know there used to be a trail here."

"Remember, don't look down. They almost always go away when they get bored."

"Yes, they do have big teeth, but I told you not to look down."

"Boy, I never heard a sound like that before. Weird!"

"No, I still don't know what happened to the bait. Now shut up and eat."

"Anybody here know what kind of track a grizzly [cougar, Sasquatch] makes?"

"Yep, I know this is a day trip. But just for the fun of it, I think we should try to build a fire and a lean-to."

"That mountain [rapid, waterfall, drop-off, rock] wasn't here last time."

"This could be bad. The sun is setting in the east."

"The moon? Ha, you must think I'm stupid. Now, what really makes the tides?"

"We had better sleep with the food. There are a lot of grizzlies around here."

"Stop complaining. When I said I had an eighty percent success rate, I was referring to the number of clients I get back to camp with."

"I don't care what your preferences are, you share a tent with Lurch."

"Look, I said I'd come back for you, and I mean it."

"Don't worry, lots of shortcuts take a lot longer than the regular trail."

"If everybody will settle down for a few moments, I will demonstrate the technique for bailing a boat with a coffee can and two thermos cups, okay?"

"Nobody run. That only excites them."

"Run!"

"Watch out for rattlesnakes [pythons, fer-de-lance, cobras, black mambas]."

"Of course I have permission for you to hunt here, but just for the heck of it crouch down behind these bushes until that tractor goes by."

"Two bits of information. Number one: We have just run

out of toilet paper! Number two: There's a lot of poison ivy around here."

"Break out the oars!"

"Okay, we got Richie's vote. Now, all those in favor of cannibalism raise your hands."

I should mention here that our guides at lunch that day also came up with a bunch of comments they claimed to have actually heard from clients. They were so ridiculous that I refuse to repeat them here. Worst of all, they attributed some of the comments to one of their regular clients. For example, they reported as true their account of how this person actually uttered an "Uh-oh!" In that person's defense, let me point out that poison ivy isn't all that easy to identify out in the wild.

The Ideal Life

For a long while during the distant time of my youth, I
thought about modeling myself after Rancid Crabtree, the
old man who lived in a slab shack back against the mountain
a quarter mile or so from our house. At the time, I lived as the
lone male in a family of surly women—my mother, my grandmother, and my sister, the Troll. My father had died when I
was six, forgetting to leave word that I was to be in charge of
the family from then on. So my mother stepped immediately
into the role of general, with Gram and the Troll as her next
in command, respectively. I had no rank at all. As matters
turned out, that was probably just as well.

The shack Rancid Crabtree lived in was built from slabs, as
I have indicated. Slabs could be obtained free from the nearest
sawmill. To make a house wall, one placed them upright on
the foundation in two facing rows, so that the cracks between
the slabs were covered by the facing slabs. This produced a
wall of solid wood eight to ten inches thick, possibly more. I
mention slab houses at some length because for numerous rea-

sons they are no longer possible. So much of life is no longer possible. I guess, in a way, that is the point of this report.

I did not really fasten on Rancid Crabtree as a role model until about age eight. For one thing, the womenfolk had it in mind that I should grow up to be a refined and educated gentleman of distinction, even though I had displayed absolutely no natural tendencies in that direction. They harped constantly about my table manners, grammar, posture, hygiene, appearance, and general grossness. Not knowing any better, I went along with their criticisms and tried to improve myself as much as possible. But nothing seemed to take.

To show just how ridiculous all this was, I will mention only one small requirement: I was expected to comb my hair every day, whether I was going out or not! "Comb that hair!" the women would shout, sometimes in unison. I realize the reader may have trouble believing that anyone could be so finicky, but they were. And it made me terribly jumpy as a young child. Never did I know from what direction the next criticism might come.

It was about this time that I became aware that a whole different kind of life was possible, namely that of Rancid Crabtree. One bitterly cold winter morning I was tromping out through the snow to wait for the school bus. The tromp was bad enough, but the fact that it led to nothing more than a day at school made it much worse. Through a gap in the trees I could see Rancid's shack over against the mountain. No smoke emanated from his chimney. This meant he was still in bed! You see, with Rancid's way of life, there was no reason to get up early, or to get up at all, if you didn't feel like it. I suspect that on occasion he stayed in bed all day simply because he couldn't think of a single good reason to get up. In fact, if he did get up in the morning he would simply have to go back to bed in the evening. So by staying in bed in the first place he achieved a major efficiency. I'm sure he thought of it in just that way, too. Rancid certainly wouldn't regard boring and irritating school as any good reason to get up. And to judge from his degree of education, he never had.

As I grew older, I began to pay closer attention to Rancid and his lifestyle. First of all, I knew that I could build myself a shack of slabs at virtually no cost. I might have to buy some land to put the shack on, but land was cheap. Still, it would require some money. I did wonder how Rancid had come up with the money to buy his forty acres of woods and mountain, but maybe he had found it. My whole concept of him would have been ruined if I learned he had actually *earned* the money.

One thing in particular that I liked about Rancid's lifestyle was that he never took baths. He warned me against baths, too. He said that soap and water would eat holes in my protective crust and allow germs to get in. My mother, who was ignorant of such scientific matters, still insisted that I take a bath twice a week. And of course Rancid was right. Every winter soap and water would eat holes in my protective crust and the germs would get in and give me a cold. Rancid, on the other hand, never got sick.

Because Rancid had no way of preserving meat, he never went hunting for deer or elk until cold weather set in. Then he would hang his game out in his woodshed and let the weather take care of it. Every November he and a friend would drive his old truck down to the Selway, where they would camp out and hunt for elk. I think God must have looked favorably upon Rancid, because that is the only reason his old truck could have made it, year after year, to the Selway and back. Rancid and his friend never failed to return with at least one elk, and usually two.

In addition to deer and elk, Rancid shot grouse, pheasants, ducks, geese, rabbits, and whatever else might reside in the woods behind his house or the bottom land of the nearby farms. If he wasn't hunting, he fished. He had an old cedar-strip boat with which he fished for kokanee and trout in Lake Blight. He caught so many fish, he would smoke them and then give most of them away to his neighbors. Despite all the demeaning jokes and comments about his character, Rancid was very popular in the neighborhood.

I have noticed over the years that a person who hunts or fishes for his food does so with a far greater intensity than one who doesn't, and I suspect that might account for Rancid's proficiency in both those activities. Personal risk can provide a quick cure for any attention deficit one might have.

The old woodsman's diet was, of course, weighted heav-ily toward protein, which current dietary research suggests may have accounted for his lean frame and good health. Each spring and fall he also picked an abundance of the wild mushrooms that sprang up in the woods behind his cabin. He would dry the mushrooms and then toss them into a five-gallon crock, until he needed them either for soup or to gar-nish his venison steak. Picking and eating wild mushrooms, by the way, is another excellent cure for attention deficit.

Rancid got his heat and fuel for cooking from firewood that he cut from dead timber in the woods behind his shack. Although the wood was free, Rancid tended to be rather frugal with it because the getting of it required an expenditure of energy. He cut the wood as he needed it, never bothering to work up a whole winter's supply at one time. This may be the reason, as I suspected, why he sometimes spent the whole day in bed. If he got up, he would either be cold all day or have to go out and cut wood.

For what cash he needed, Rancid ran a trapline each winter for skunks, weasels (ermine), muskrats, martin, and anything else that had a price on its hide. He was regarded as one of the best trappers in our part of the country. I don't know how much money Rancid made from trapping but, as with every other part of his life, whatever he got was enough. Come to think of it, that may have been the secret to his success.

Rancid didn't have a radio or subscribe to any magazines or newspapers, and he cared nothing about either the national or local news, although he did enjoy a choice bit of gossip from time to time. I don't know what Rancid did for entertainment in the evening, except maybe stare at the fire burning its way through his old barrel stove. I do know that the holes in the stove did put on a rather nice light show in the dark of night. Also, sometimes a spark would fly out and set fire to the shack, thereby creating a break in any monotony that may have set in.

So there it was, the ideal lifestyle. I recognized it as such when I was only eight years old. During most of my years of sitting in schoolrooms, I often daydreamed about how nice it would be to live in a little shack back in the mountains and do nothing all day but hunt and fish and maybe, in winter, run a trapline. I spent a great deal of time training myself to do all those things because I couldn't wait to be free of the womenfolk who controlled my life at home and insisted, even against all odds, that I grow up to be a responsible and productive human being. But little did Mom, Gram, and the Troll know of my plans for a Rancid life, so free and lovely and wonderful, with all the time in the world to fish and hunt and spend exactly as I wished!

Then one day Melba Peachbottom, the prettiest girl in Delmore Blight Junior High, actually spoke to me. She said, "I love the way your hair is always combed so nice. Would you like to carry my books?"

A Creek Too Far

Lou was first to arrive at the rendezvous point, a broad gravel beach where the stream rippled down into a darkly quiet pool dimpled with rising fish. *Nice*, he thought. He slipped out of his vest and hung it on a limb conveniently protruding up from a driftwood log. The log also provided him with a seat while he pulled off his waders. He snapped smaller branches from the log, whittled some shavings, and soon had a fire crackling away. He leaned back against a limb and propped his feet up on a rock next to the fire. *This is the life*, he thought. A soft breeze carried the smoke away from him but he could still catch its fragrance. Cedar. Nothing like the smell of cedar smoke, the best perfume in the world.

Jack and Fred came wandering in. "Thought you'd have our dinner on by now," Fred said.

"Got the fire going, didn't I?" Lou said. "Just waiting for you guys to bring in the fish."

"Where's your fish?" Jack said. "Bet you didn't catch any."

"Oh, I caught plenty. Just didn't keep any. To tell you the truth, this is the best fishing I've ever had."

"You can say that again," Fred agreed. "I don't know why we've never fished here before. It is absolutely fantastic! But one of us should have kept some fish for supper."

"Don't worry about it," Lou said. "We've got some nice thick steaks to grill."

"Terrific!" Jack said. "Anyway, the reason we never fished here before is we didn't know about it. I don't reckon many people do. I never saw a track all day."

"Me, neither," Lou said. "But, hey, don't knock it!"

"Anyone for a shot of bourbon while the steaks are cooking?" Fred asked, hauling out a flask. It was generally agreed that that was Fred's best idea since the trip began. After disposing of the steaks as well as roasted potatoes and corn on the cob, both dribbling with real butter, the three friends sat around the fire smoking cigars and sipping bourbon. *This is the life*, Lou thought for the umpteenth time that day.

"It sure is," Jack said.

"What is?" Lou said.

"The life," Fred said.

Lou blew out a stream of cigar smoke. "What do you mean, 'the life'?"

"You said, 'This is the life,' " Fred said. "And all I said was, 'It sure is'!"

Lou shook his head. "I didn't say 'This is the life,' I *thought* it!"

"No, you said it," Jack said. "How could we hear you if you only thought it?"

"You guys are starting to scare me," Lou said. "No more bourbon for either of you."

"No more for you, either," Fred said. "You're starting to think out loud, for pity's sake. Pretty soon you're gonna be wandering about town telling jokes to yourself and laughing because this is the first time you've heard them."

That night as he lay in his sleeping bag Lou wondered if he might actually be slipping a little. Maybe he was beginning to think out loud. He hoped not. It was the sort of thing that could ruin your social life pretty darn fast. Come to think of it, he didn't have all that much of a social life anyway. He lay there staring up at the stars, trying not to think anything in case Jack or Fred was still awake.

The next morning they were up at first light, stuffing themselves with bacon and eggs and hash browns and onions with gravy and buttered toast. Lou was still trying not to think anything as they sat around the fire after breakfast having a third cup of coffee. Lou suddenly thought that it was the best coffee he'd ever tasted. He could have kicked himself as soon as he realized he'd thought something, but neither of his friends seemed to have noticed.

"Too bad Barney ain't along," Fred said. "He always enjoys these trips. Come to think of it, I haven't seen him lately. He retire or what?"

"Died," Jack said. "Barney died."

"No!" Lou said. "I never heard."

"Me, neither," Fred said. "Geez, ol' Barney's gone. Now, there was a guy knew how to fish."

Lou nodded. "He sure did. The guy was pure magic with a fly rod. Barney would have loved this stream, I can tell you that. You sure he died, Jack?"

"Pretty sure. Made it a whole lot easier to bury him."

"That's usually a good sign."

"What was it, an accident?" Lou asked.

"Naw, he just worked too hard the last few years. Doc Mosby told me the official cause was heart attack, but the real cause was a deficiency of fishing."

"Well, I know one thing," Lou said. "I'm going to make sure that doesn't happen to me, a deficiency of fishing."

"Me, too," said Fred.

"One thing's for sure," Jack said. "There ain't any of us three going to keel over from working too hard."

"No kidding," Lou said. "Or from working at all!"

They had a big laugh over that. Every once in a while Lou got off a good one.

Although it was almost beyond their imagination, the fishing that day turned out to be even better than the day before, with the trout bigger, hungrier, and feistier. This time they each kept a couple for their supper. Lou fried them in butter and the bacon grease left over from breakfast. Afterward, they once again sat around the fire sipping bourbon and smoking cigars.

"Man, this is my idea of heaven," Jack mused. "I don't think I'd ever tire of this."

"It's nice," Fred said. "I tell you, guys, this trip has been great therapy for me. I feel like I'm sixteen again."

"That goes for me, too," said Lou. "Only problem is, I don't know half as much now!"

They laughed till they cried over that one. Here it was, only the second day of the trip, and already Lou had got off two good ones.

"I think I figured something out, guys," Jack said, wiping away tears of mirth. "I think I know why nobody else seems to be fishing this stream."

"I hope you ain't going to say 'because it's closed,'" Lou said. "That's what occurred to me."

"No, it's because it isn't on any map. See, we were headed up to Canyon Creek, right? Well, I studied the map pretty darn close before we started, and there's no creek this size anywhere near Canyon Creek."

Lou glanced this way and that while he did the theme from *The Twilight Zone*.

"Well, shoot," Fred said. "Maybe *this* is Canyon Creek, you ever think of that?"

"Well, duh," Jack said. "Don't you think that a creek called Canyon Creek just might be in a canyon?"

"Could be, I suppose, if you want to get technical."

"Somewhere along the way," Jack continued, "we took a wrong turn. I figure we got to be twenty or thirty miles from where we intended to be."

"Maybe," Lou said. "But don't you remember, Jack, at one point we did drive alongside a canyon?"

"That's right," Fred said. "And you said, 'I sure hope we don't meet a logging truck on one of these narrow roads.' And right then a logging truck came around a curve."

"Yeah," Lou said. "And that's when the cigar popped out of your mouth and landed in your lap."

A thoughtful silence came over the three men as they sat there next to the fire. They peered at the peaceful stream flowing by. After a bit, Jack said, "You guys happen to notice that even with each of us sitting on a different side of this campfire, the smoke never gets in anyone's eyes?"

"What just occurred to me," said Fred, "is that we never see any tracks along the stream. Guys, *we* are supposed to leave tracks!"

"Another thing," Jack added. "I don't recall us bringing any steaks along on this trip."

"I don't, either," Fred said. "And I seem to know what either of you says before you say it."

Lou snorted. "You guys are something else. There's a simple explanation for all that stuff. For example, Fred knows what we're going to say before we say it because he's heard us say the same stuff a thousand times. And as for all the rest of it, there's a simple explanation for that, too. Here comes Barney."

The Perfect Hunt

Nearing total exhaustion from my janitorial labors, I plopped my nineteen-year-old bones down in the cushy leather office chair of Dr. Seymour Slick, dean of science. Had I been of a thoughtful nature, I might at that moment have reflected that the way of life I so desperately clung to no longer existed for me. I was now a student and a janitor at a university. That other life was gone. Vanished. Evaporated. Had being in denial existed back then, I would have been a classic case of it. I simply couldn't believe that my former life had slipped away like a thief in the night, taking all the good silver.

Consider a school day from my former life: I'm seventeen, a junior in high school. It's four o'clock in the morning. Jim Russell, Norm Nelson, and I are in Jim's big old blue sedan heading out to hunt deer in a distant swamp. Three hours later we're back at my house, a deer strapped to a fender. By nine-thirty I'm in English class, wrestling with Julius Caesar, and losing. (It's a wonderful life, but, hey, nothing's perfect.) That afternoon I get off the school bus, stroll into my house, pick up my shotgun, a box of shells, a brace of freshly baked cinnamon rolls, and a few menacing gestures from my grandmother. Minutes later I'm down on the creek hunting pheasants, grouse, quail, ducks, and any other ingredient of a mixed bag. It's all so wonderful I never even suspect it won't last forever. Then, suddenly, without warning, disaster strikes: I'm thrust into college!

Slumped in Dean Slick's chair, my feet propped on his desk, I remained locked in the delusion that I was simply living a much more inconvenient extension of my old life. I picked up the phone and dialed the president's office. "Yeah?" a voice yawned. It was my old buddy Retch Sweeney, student janitor in the Administration Building.

"You ready?" I asked.

"Yup. Gotta dump the prez's wastebaskets, then I'm outta here. See you at the truck."

I hung up the phone and started to extract myself from the dean's chair, but the soft, creamy leather held me like a magnet. *So this is what it's like to be rich*, I thought. The gleaming, if somewhat dusty, desktop had about the same square footage as my dorm room. It was completely clear except for two photographs. One was of an attractive, silver-haired lady; his wife, I supposed. The other photo, much larger, was of himself. He was crouched in snow, one hand holding a rifle, the other resting possessively on the massive rack of a spectacular mule deer. The dean appeared typically stern. Possibly he hadn't shot the deer at all but stopped it cold with one of his steely glares, then pierced its heart with a bolt of sarcasm.

Retch was gunning the motor of his pickup by the time I arrived. We cleared the city limits well after ten. The mountains were more than a hundred miles away, our intended camp much farther. Snow was beginning to fall.

"Starting to snow," I said. "Good thing you got at least one good windshield wiper, Retch."

"Yeah. Too bad it's not on the driver's side."

"Did you find a spare tire?"

"Yeah, several, but they were moving too fast for me to get a lug wrench on."

"This snow is good," I said. "We'll have some good tracking."

We had gone out every weekend for a month without seeing a buck. They wouldn't be able to hide from us now, not with the snow. Hunters climb a mountain of expectation—the next time, the next turn, the next rise—and they never ever get to the top, although I was beginning to think I could see it.

We reached our campsite well after midnight. During the week we had imagined this moment: erecting the tent, its canvas straining tautly against its poles; building the campfire, feeding it fuzz sticks until the orange flames danced up and drove back the night. We would have a couple of forked sticks holding a spit over the fire, and we would heat up chili in a pot hanging from the spit, and roast some hot dogs to go with the chili, and we'd sit around the fire afterward and tell all the old stories and laugh ourselves sick.

"I'm beat," Retch said. "Let's just spread the tent on the ground and shove our stuff into it."

"Okay," I said. "Care for a cold wiener before we turn in?"

One of these times, I thought, *maybe we'll actually pitch the tent.*

I have been trying to think of a single word that might describe these hunts that we squeezed into our college weekends, but *ragged* is the only thing that comes to mind.

They were thrown together out of scraps of time, energy, and longing for something already gone and never to return.

The next morning was bitter cold. As I lay in the flat tent staring at canvas an inch from my eyes, I suddenly realized that the zipper on my sleeping bag had frozen shut. Only heat from a roaring fire could possibly thaw it loose. Just as I started to cry out for help, I heard Retch stir.

"Get up and build a fire," he grunted. "Otherwise, I'll have to shoot you."

And he called that a threat. Ha!

Retch peeked out from under the frozen canvas to assess the degree of pain required to get up and build a fire. "Cripes!" he hissed.

"That bad?" I croaked.

"No," he whispered. "There's a gigantic buck standing right in camp. Hand me a rifle."

I rummaged around until I found a rifle and a handful of shells and gave them to Retch, even as I pondered why a deer would be standing in our camp. Maybe he simply couldn't believe what he saw.

"Dang," Retch said. "He just stepped behind that spruce tree." He slid out of the tent on his belly, wearing only his faded-red long johns. I peeked out. Retch was now up and tiptoeing barefoot through the snow, circling out around the tree, rifle already at his shoulder. I waited for the shot. That deer was as good as in the locker. But no! Now Retch was tiptoeing behind the spruce. One button on his seat flap had come undone. *Cripes,* I thought, *what is wrong with this picture?* All my life I had created images in my head of The Perfect Hunt. This wasn't one of them.

Minutes passed. No shot. I waited, tense with expectation. And waited. Finally Retch came stomping back through the snow. "He dropped down into the canyon," he growled.

"Didn't even have the decency to give me a single shot. And not only did I freeze my feet, I froze my—!"

"Stop," I said. "I don't want to hear. But hey, as long as you're up, you might as well build the fire."

As our eyes sifted the carbon particles out of the smoke from our smoldering campfire, Retch and I sullenly consumed a breakfast of cowboy coffee (boil one cowboy), chili-warmed-in-the-can (our own recipe), and wieners flambé. Not once did we feel the urge to tell an old story or laugh ourselves silly.

We spent the morning hunting the mountaintop. We found plenty of tracks, but all of them seemed to be headed off down into the steep and, with the snow, treacherous canyon.

As we stood staring down into the canyon, an old rancher drove up. "That's right, boys," he confirmed. "These deer hang out down by the river during the day. Then they start moving back up about an hour or so before dark."

"I guess our best bet is to head off down into the canyon and see if we can take them by surprise," I said.

"I reckon." He pointed at our rifles. "Particularly with them peep sights. Most of the shooting done from the ridge here is at real long range. Now, that couple over there has got the right idea for hunting this country."

He pointed back along the ridge road to a large white pickup. A tall, slender man and a silver-haired woman were setting up a table on the edge of the ridge. "They come up here one afternoon every hunting season and set up their table. They build themselves a nice campfire and put a grill over it and a pot of coffee on. Then they sit at the table and play cards with each other and snack on a few treats. About the time the deer start up out of the canyon, they scope the herds out until each of them picks out a nice buck. They got custom-built rifles, their own hand-loaded ammo, and scopes the size of salamis. After they make their pick, they fire off one shot apiece. The trajectories could skim dust off a chalk line for half a mile. I then take a couple packhorses down, field-dress the deer, haul 'em out, and load 'em on their pickup. While I'm doin' that they throw three thick steaks on the grill. After I'm done tidying up, we sit around the fire, eat dinner, and have a couple of drinks. Tell a few old stories, too. Laugh ourselves silly sometimes."

"Slick!" I said.

"Dang tootin' it's slick," the rancher said.

"No, I mean that's Dr. Seymour Slick, dean of science at the university."

"Oh, right you are, son. By the way, before you head off down into the canyon, you better switch those tennis shoes for your boots. And put on some warmer clothes. It'll be pretty cold by the time you get back up to the ridge."

"Sure," I said. There was no point in explaining to him that we were already wearing our "boots" and all the clothes we owned.

The first step into the canyon was a long one but we somehow managed to skid to a stop before breaking the sound barrier. Then we inched down the rest of the way. We spent the rest of the afternoon irritating the deer but never putting any of them at serious risk.

Along toward evening, we heard two shots, one right after the other. I peered up at the ridge. Two elongated dots stood next to the big white pickup. Several horses were headed down a trail.

It was dark before we made it up out of the canyon. The white pickup was still there. Sounds of laughter drifted over from around the campfire. Retch and I plodded up to say hello. The old rancher leaped out of a camp chair and came toward us, an iced drink in one hand.

"By golly, you fellas made quite a trek. Didn't hear a shot, so I expect you didn't get one. If you had, I'd have hauled it up for nothin'. Ain't often I see a couple of hunters that dedicated."

"Thanks," I said.

Dr. Slick stepped forward. "Why, it's none other than McManus and Sweeney! Sarah, come meet these young men. They're the dots we watched all afternoon traipsing up and down the canyon. You know, fellas, when you waded up to your waists across that icy river, I said to myself, that's a good move. It will surprise the deer because they'll think a hunter would have to be crazy to wade that river. I have to tell you, I envied you two dots this afternoon. There was a time when I hunted that way myself, and it is truly the way to hunt. It's not just shooting, it's real hunting. It's what I like to think of as the perfect hunt."

"Gee, thanks, Dr. Slick," Retch said. "You're certainly welcome to hunt with us anytime."

Dr. Slick's face brightened at the thought, and he gave Retch a big beaming grin.

"Not in a thousand years," he said.

Thirty Days

He had fished every day for thirty days straight, each day on a different stream. On the last day, his friend Doc Patterson stopped by in the evening to congratulate him.

"So, you did it," Doc said.

"Yep," Bill Malone said. "Thirty streams in thirty days."

"Which one today, Canyon Creek?"

"I didn't do Canyon Creek."

"I should have known," Doc said. "A nasty piece of work, that Canyon Creek."

"You're telling me," Bill said. "Some nice fish in there, though. Probably never seen an artificial. I suppose because most people aren't dumb enough to risk it."

"There's a place for dumb in fishing," Doc said.

"Yeah, well, in the future when I need any dumb, I'll make sure to take Charlie Smith with me."

"Couldn't make a better choice, if you're looking for dumb."

"Yeah," Bill said, "but to give Charlie his due, he at least got me out of the office for a month. Tell you the truth, I was getting a little stressed out from all the work."

"It's good to get away," Doc said. "Do a little fishing. Or, in your case, a lot of fishing. Must have been nice to get back to all your favorite streams. Which one did you start on?"

Bill had started his fishing marathon on Sand Creek, the creek of his youth, and, appropriately, the first creek he had ever fished. Sand Creek was now technically a crick. It wound mostly through cow pastures, and the cows had done what they could, which was quite a lot, to turn the creek into a crick. The farmers had done their part, too, by dumping old farm implements and junk cars into it from time to time, using the excuse that their intent was to protect the banks from erosion, not to rid themselves of worn-out wagons and cars.

The first time his father had taken him to fish Sand Creek it was still a creek, thick with brush on both banks and crisscrossed with fallen trees and beaver dams, and on each side were fields of huge blackened stumps, some of them as large as houses. His father put him up on his shoulders and fought through the brush and found a log for them to sit on and they had hauled out trout after trout, sparkling like tiny rainbows in the sunlight. They filled a milk bucket halfway up with little fish, the limit in those days being all you could catch. Shortly after that first fishing trip, a government agency of some kind got the idea that it should clean up the creek. Crews of men and machines soon arrived and cleared away the brush and logs and beaver dams. From then on there were a lot fewer fish in the creek. Then the cows showed up and finished turning the creek into a crick.

Bill hadn't fished Sand Creek in twenty-five years, but it hadn't changed in the slightest since then. He dropped over the hill at the old Russell place, just as he had done so many times before. He dug some worms out of the potato patch down next to the creek, and put the worms in an old tin Band-Aid can that was perfect for worms and prized by kids in his day. Then he worked his way upstream, hole by hole, up past the confluences of Little Sand and Schweitzer creeks, and all the events of his long association with the creek came flooding back in vivid detail.

When he reached the Haverstead farm, he waded across the creek, the water cold and swift, rising above his knees before he reached the far bank. He found the old trail right where it had always been, and he followed it up the hill and through the woods to the road, stopping briefly along the way to pick and eat a handful of dewberries from the tangle of vines that still matted the ancient brush pile.

"Gosh, Sand Creek," Doc said. "I haven't fished Sand Creek since before I went off to college. It was still good, hunh?"

"Yeah, it was real good. I would have taken you with me if I could've, Doc."

"Hey, some of us got to work, you know. Not everybody gets a month's vacation to do nothing but fish. I expect you did Deep Creek. Those rocks slick as ever?"

"Yep, slicker than a stockbroker in a bear market. But I fished all the way from the railroad trestle up to Bob and Babe's Bar and never took a spill. Went in and quaffed a couple of cool ones. Same old crowd, just like the old days, loggers mostly, wrapping up their day. And were they ever glad to see me!"

"Bob and Babe still alive?"

"Sure. People like them don't ever die. And they all still love my stories. I'm not exaggerating, Doc, they laughed till they cried. I told them the time you and I were fishing Deep Creek and racing each other through the water to get to that good hole, and I slipped on some of those rocks and went down and cracked my tailbone. Hurt so bad I just stiffened out straight as a board and sank to the bottom. And what did you do, being a doctor and all? You made at least three casts right over the top of me. I know because I was peering up through the water at you."

"I'll have you to understand, my good man, that I was following the prescribed medical treatment for a busted tailbone, which is to soak it in ice water for a minute or two immediately after the fall. You expect me to stand there and do nothing the whole while you're soaking your tailbone? With big cutthroat rising in a good hole?"

"Speaking of cold water," Bill said, "I fished Boulder Creek a couple days ago. You remember that spring up on Boulder Creek? Water about one degree north of ice. Well, I drove up to the spring and put a can of brew in it. Then I drove all the way back to the old trapper's cabin and fished upstream toward the spring. You've probably forgotten that principle of serious angling: Always fish toward the brew and not away from it."

"That principle had slipped my mind," Doc said. "I'm glad you reminded me of both it and the spring, because I'm going to fish Boulder Creek this weekend. Ha!"

"No!"

"Yes! Now tell me about the other streams you fished in thirty days."

"They were all great," Bill said. "Too bad you couldn't have been there."

"I could have been there," Doc said. "If you'd wanted me."

"Yeah, right, and I'm about to do that, hunh? Now, let's see, some of the other streams were the Snow, Pack, Ruby, Callahan, Lightning, Trout, Fisher, Grouse, and—"

"Tell me again about Canyon Creek," Doc said. "I love it!"

"Well, as you might suspect, I didn't go back to Canyon Creek this time. Charlie and I were up there earlier."

"When was that?"

"About a month ago."

"And?"

"You know Charlie, he's practically a mountain goat. So we're down there in the canyon and have caught and released probably twenty really nice fish apiece. But it gets dark early down in there, and I tell Charlie we better hike back out of the canyon. He says, 'No, we can fish another hour and then climb out.' Against my better judgment I say, 'Okay, I guess we can do that.' Getting along toward evening, we start climbing out and get up a good ways when we come to a big gap in the ledge we're on. Charlie jumps across."

"Yeah, he's half goat, all right," Doc said. "I'm not sure if it's the bottom half or the top half, though. So what happened next?"

"That's what I'm not sure of. The last thing I remember is Charlie yelling, 'Go for it, Bill, you can make it!'"

"That Charlie is so dumb."

"Yeah, almost as dumb as me! Anyway, Doc, when do you think I can get out of this full-body cast?"

"How long's it been now?"

"Thirty days."

"Right," Doc said. "Oh, I reckon you'll be out of the cast in a couple of weeks. Give you enough time to work in a dozen hunts."

Where's Mr. Sun?

I've always enjoyed reading about science, but I'm going to give up discussing the subject with my so-called friends. For one thing, it can be dangerous.

I'm not talking about the time the young fellow I had working for me said, "I wonder what makes the tides."

"The moon makes the tides," I told him.

He laughed. "You must think I'm pretty stupid, pulling my leg like that. Really, what makes the tides?"

That sort of response merely makes your mind go blank. It leaves no room for discussion. What I'm getting at here are subtler points of science.

Oh, yes, and another thing I'm not going to do anymore: get up at two o'clock in the morning to go fishing. That's how this whole business got started.

Actually, we left at two o'clock, so I'm not sure exactly when I got up. Probably about five minutes to two, so I'd have some time for preparation.

The four of us were in Mort's car: Mort, Retch, Henry, and

myself. Mort was driving. We were using Mort's car because we had all decided that Mort owned the best fishing car by far. Mort was obviously pleased to have the best fishing car. It was his first fishing trip with the rest of us, and nobody had bothered to inform him that the three reasons his car was best for fishing were (1) it had a motor; (2) it had four wheels; and (3) it belonged to Mort, not any of the rest of us. The Boulder River Road was one of the worst around.

The stretch of the Boulder we like to fish best lies up against the east side of the Snowy range of the Rockies. This accounts for its long twilight period, which is important to a proper understanding of this report.

"Look at that moon up there," Retch said at one point as we drove along. "Beautiful." Then he added thoughtfully: "I wonder what holds it up."

Most people, fishermen in particular, would simply let this statement go, regarding it as nothing more than an expression of appreciation. But I, being a science buff of sorts, have to go and respond. "Well, probably its orbital speed along a rut formed in space. Kind of like spinning the ball on a roulette table, except the moon doesn't slow down enough to fall out of the rut."

"Rut in space?" Retch said. "I don't see no rut in space."

"Yeah," said Henry. "How can you have a rut in space?"

"It's just space," Mort said. "A bunch of nothing."

"Not so fast, numskulls," I responded. "Einstein pretty much proved that space is something."

"Yeah, it's something," Retch said. "It's space."

"A bunch of nothing," Henry said. "I could prove that myself. You see anything between us and the moon?"

"Yes, but . . ." I started to say.

"Right, whatcha see is a bunch of nothing," Mort said.

"I give up," I said. "I suppose you fellas all believe it's an absolute certainty that the sun will rise in the morning."

A big laugh.

"Well, yeah," Retch said. "Otherwise, I wouldn't have bothered bringing my sunglasses!"

This got another big laugh.

"Well, it is not an absolute certainty," I tried to explain. "It's only a very high probability."

"Like one hundred percent probable," Henry said.

"Just because the sun has come up every day for the last hundred billion years or so doesn't mean that it will come up tomorrow," I said, ignoring the raucous shouts. Nevertheless, as we were later to learn, this simple statement put the idea in their heads that one morning the sun just might not come up. It must also be remembered that I was here dealing with intellects the size of neutrinos.

We eventually arrived at Henry's cabin, got our stuff moved in, and by first light were out on the river in the delicate process of distinguishing a rock bump on the bottom from the strike of a steelhead. We returned to the cabin for lunch and were out on the river again by one o'clock. But we were beginning to fade. By two o'clock Mort had disappeared.

"Anybody seen Mort?" I asked.

"Probably slipped back to camp and is drinking up all our brew," Retch said.

After further conjecture, this possibility was turned into a probability. We immediately rushed back to the cabin, only to discover Mort asleep on the hillside, his hat over his eyes. Only two empties rested nearby, allaying our suspicions that Mort had undertaken a serious raid on our supply of brew.

Now, it is probable that there are some people in the world who can come upon a person sleeping out alone and are not compelled to commit a practical joke on him. Retch and Henry are not members of that group.

Scarcely do they realize that Mort is fast asleep than they

have a plan in place. Indeed, one might easily suspect that they had been planning for just this opportunity for many months.

With no apparent communication between them, they instantly rushed to the cabin and hauled out tent pegs and wooden stakes, anything that could be pounded into the ground, and they pounded in a virtual fence around the dozing Mort. Then they wound fishing line from stake to stake and peg to peg, until Mort was enmeshed in a virtual net. I watched with some interest, realizing, of course, that Retch and Henry could not help themselves. It is what they do.

The work had been hard and apparently rewarding, but afterward Henry said, "Whew, I'm beat."

"Me, too," said Retch. "I think we should all go take a nap ourselves."

It was thus decided that we three would go to the cabin and sack out for an hour or so and wake up refreshed enough to fish the evening bite. Even more likely, it was assumed, we would be awakened by a roar from Mort.

Time passed. The sun slipped behind the mountains and the long twilight settled in. Mort awakened and was immediately enraged, not by the net that had been formed around him, it later turned out, but by the fact that his friends had allowed him *to sleep outside all night*, when he easily could have been eaten by wandering creatures of the dark. This was the fundamental mistake. Mort assumed it was now an early, predawn morning! He stripped away the feeble line and pegs, grabbed his rod, and headed upstream to go fishing. It being early morning, as he thought, it was natural to expect the day to grow ever brighter.

As it happened, Mort got into the evening bite and soon had one steelhead after another hitting his lure. After he had released his third fish, he stood up, stretched, rubbed his back, and looked around. The "morning" had grown darker. He glanced at the eastern sky. Clear. *Wait a second*, he thought, as only Mort could, *the sun should be up by now*. He glanced at his watch. It was nearly eight. The sun had failed to rise! He dropped his rod and took off in a dead run for the cabin, hoping to share his panic.

Mort burst into the cabin. "The sun is gone!" he shouted. "The sun is gone!"

Three pairs of feet instantly hit the floor.

"What do you mean the sun is gone?" I asked. "The sun is supposed to be gone. It's night. We overslept!"

"No, you dirty rats let me sleep out all night," Mort yelled back. "But I forgive you, 'cause we're all going to die anyway!"

"Holy cow," Retch said, glancing at his watch. "He's right, we did sleep all night! It's already half past eight in the morning! And the sun ain't up!"

"Geez," said Henry, staring at the floor. "And here I had decided to get married someday and have children. Now the sun don't come up!"

"Wait a second," I said. "The sun always comes up."

"You said it yourself," Retch said. "You read all those science books and everything and they say it's only probable that the sun will come up. And now it hasn't!"

"I must have been lying," I said. "I think the sun always comes up and . . . But what's that?" I pointed at the sky. "It's the moon! It's nighttime! You imbeciles scared me half to death!"

We drove home a couple of nights later, but I think all of us had a new appreciation of the sunrise. I know I did. Otherwise, why do we stand out in the yard and blow kisses at the sun each morning?

There was still one thing I wondered about, though: What really does keep the moon up there?

The Lucky Guy

Retch Sweeney and I pulled into Fenton Quagmire's expansive driveway and stopped in front of his five-car garage. It was four A.M. The house was dark.

"Just as I suspected," Retch growled. "Quagmire has forgotten all about our hunting trip. Good!"

"Why good?" I said.

"It's not that Quagmire—after you—is the most forgetful guy in the world. It's not that—after you—he is the most incompetent. It's that he's the luckiest. He drives downtown, Quagmire will find not one but two empty parking spots right together smack-dab in front of his destination. He finds two parking spots because Quagmire is so incompetent he can't manage to park in just one! You go fishing with him, the fish are always on his side of the boat! You use exactly the same tackle and everything, and he catches all the fish. I can't stand it!"

I shook my head in disbelief. "Fenton can't be all that lucky. Here he's slept in on the first day of deer season. He'll make us all late for opening day! Honk your horn!"

Retch laughed maniacally. "No way. Quagmire deserves a little bad luck for being so forgetful. We're outta here."

He backed the truck out of the driveway and roared off down the road. Two hours later, we were peering through the dim light of early dawn, trying to follow game trails over the top of Mount Misery. Had the mountain been nameless, we probably would have called it Misery ourselves. Although we had extracted a number of deer and elk from its canyons and forests and precipitous side hills, we had suffered much misery in doing so. I recall that once a benevolent four-wheel-drive truck broke through the ice on a large mud puddle, thereby enabling me to scoop up enough water for a pot of coffee. We sifted the pebbles out with our teeth. Unfortunately, that was by no means the low point of the trip. I don't even want to think about the low point. But Retch and I were young then, and dumb. Now we were no longer young. Late in the afternoon we rendezvoused in a little clearing atop the mountain. That in itself was a bit of success. Usually we didn't find each other again until sometime after dark, if then.

"See anything?" he asked.

"Nope. You?"

"The freshest tracks I saw had little trees growing in them. I don't know what's happened to the deer. Too bad you didn't want to bring Quagmire, Pat. At least he would have had one by now and be sitting in the car reading a book. You should be ashamed of yourself. The guy is lucky. Maybe a little of his luck would have rubbed off on us."

"I'm sorry," I said. "I don't know what I could have been thinking. Anyway, I'm tired of hunting deer where there aren't any. Besides that, we'll have used up a perfectly good Saturday for nothing. Let's head back to town."

"Okay by me," Retch said. "I just hope Quagmire isn't too

mad at you for not bringing him along. But what the heck, when I see him I'll try to smooth things over between yous."

"Hey, what are friends for?" I said.

We headed back down the mountain. As we were passing one of the ranches that spread across the foothills, we came upon Quagmire's Humvee parked just off the road. We turned in and parked alongside it. There was no sign of Fenton.

"You suppose he's all right?" Retch said.

"Sure," I said. "He's lucky."

"I suppose. How come Quagmire has a Humvee and we go hunting in my old pickup truck?"

"The Humvee is new. Obviously, Quagmire doesn't want to get it dirty. You would be the same way."

"No, I wouldn't. I'd be tearing out through a swamp someplace."

Presently, Quagmire came strolling out of the woods with a rifle over his shoulder. "Boy, am I ever glad to see you two guys."

"Well, geez, Quagmire, we waited forever for you to wake up," Retch told him. "Finally, Pat insisted we take off."

"Sorry about that, old chaps. I came in late from a date and I guess I didn't even hear the alarm. Anyway, I've got a big buck down back there in the woods, and I figured if I found you guys you could help me drag it out."

Retch gave me a look. He turned back to Quagmire. "Probably a state record at least."

"Not this time, I'm afraid. Oh, probably in the top five, though."

The ranch, surrounded by about ten miles of white fence, was posted with a No Trespassing sign every fifty yards or so. "You know, Fenton," I said, "that's private property you've been hunting on."

"Indeed it is," he said. "Probably why it's such good hunting. Well, I might as well tell you what happened. It's kind of embarrassing."

Quagmire went on to explain that he had been driving along, looking for Retch's pickup truck, when a couple of nice bucks bounded across the road next to the ranch. He decided that if deer were so prevalent in the area, he had better uncase his rifle. He pulled over into a turnout and began getting set up for his hunt. In so doing he discovered that he had mistakenly grabbed a box of the wrong shells in his rush to catch up with us.

"Just my luck," he said. "Here I'd been so looking forward to my hunt with you two chaps, and then I do a stupid thing like that."

To go on with his tale of woe: While Quagmire was standing there pondering his bad luck and stupidity, a shiny new Chevy Suburban came zipping out of the ranch. It was, of course, driven by an attractive young woman. She stopped and asked Quagmire if he was in trouble. Fenton shyly explained his bad luck and stupidity. Well, it turned out that her father had taken up gunsmithing as a hobby many years ago, and at that moment she was taking one of his custom-made .270s to the Silver Spoon Country Club to be auctioned off at a special affair that evening. The rifle was accompanied by several boxes of hand-loaded shells, each marked for a particular range and game animal. She told Quagmire he could borrow the gun and some shells if he'd return them to the country club in time for the auction that evening.

"Also, it's getting a little late in the day," she said. "Maybe you should hunt right here on the ranch."

"You sure that would be all right?" Quagmire said.

"Certainly. Not only am I young and beautiful, but I own this ranch and two others just like it. By the way, you aren't married, are you?"

"Not at the moment," Quagmire said.

"Well, in that case, why don't you join me for dinner at the country club?"

Quagmire leaned wearily against Retch's old truck. "Can you believe it? Now I've got to go to dinner at a stuffy old country club, just because I didn't take the time to make sure I had the right shells. So, anyway, I must be off, if I'm to make it to dinner on time. If you chaps would be so nice as to drag my deer out and drop it off at Axle's Meat Cutters, I'd appreciate it."

"No problem," I said.

That evening, as Retch and I were hauling Quagmire's deer into Axle's Meat Cutters, neither of us talked much. Finally, Retch said, "I just don't understand what beautiful women see in Quagmire."

"I don't either," I said. "He's handsome, rich, intelligent, and charming, but otherwise, nothing."

"Yeah," Retch said. "I guess he's just lucky."

Many Are Called

While doing research in basic physics and plane geometry down at Duffy's Pool Hall the other day, I ran into a chap named Vinnie. I'd met him a few times before but he hung out mostly with his own crowd at Duffy's, guys who seemed to be in the banking business, loans and that sort of thing, or so I've judged from overhearing bits of their conversation. I guess that Vinnie, a big, beefy fellow, might once have been a professional fighter, what with his scars and all.

Vinnie laughed. "Naw, I'm kind of a businessman. Got what you call a, uh, a finance business."

"Brokerage?" I said.

"Oh, yeah, there's some of that, but only as a last resort, mind you."

When he wandered over to talk with me, I was afraid he might want to discuss business. I know absolutely nothing about business, let alone finance or anything involving numbers. Higher math to me is anything with triple digits.

So I was pleased to learn that Vinnie only wanted to talk fishing.

"Hey, guy," he said, "I hear you got quite a rep as one of them fly-fishermen."

I gave a modest chuckle. "Well, to tell you the truth, Vinnie, I'm not all that great."

"I know, that's your rep, not so great, but I figured you might give me some pointers about how to get started in fly-fishin' anyway. You see, this business I'm in gets kinda, uh, stressful, and I hear fly-fishin' is supposed to be real relaxin'. Sounds like the sort of thing I could get real good at."

"Well, that depends," I said. "How old are you, Vinnie?"

"Forty-two."

I did some rapid calculations and then shook my head. "I'm sorry, Vinnie, but you're too old."

"What do you mean, too old? You tellin' me forty-two is too old?"

"That's what I'm telling you. If you started fly-fishing right now, by the time you got real good you'd be too feeble and shaky to pick up a fly, let alone a rod."

"Let alone a rod, hunh! That could be real bad in my line of work. Well, maybe you could just tell me what you know about this fly-fishin' and let me decide."

"Okay, if you've got half an hour to spare I can do that right now."

"You mean you can teach me everything you know about fly-fishin' in half an hour?"

"Give or take," I said.

"But I want to know enough about it to catch fish."

"You want to catch fish, Vinnie? The first thing I'll do, then, is correct a common misunderstanding. Fly-fishing is not about catching fish."

"It isn't? I thought it was. I thought the reason you tossed out a fly was so a fish'd come along and glom it."

"Nope. Now, that doesn't mean you won't from time to time accidentally hook a fish. But then you release it."

"You release it? But I wanna eat it!"

"Oh, goodness me, no, you don't get to eat it. Fly-fishing isn't about eating, either. You catch a fish, you release it."

"You puttin' me on? You better not be puttin' me on!"

"I wouldn't think of it, Vinnie. No, this is the straight stuff. You see, because you release any fish you catch, there's really no point in actually catching one in the first place. But sometimes it can't be helped. Let's say a fish does glom your fly and you have to haul it in and release it. One glom isn't so bad, but occasionally fish will repeatedly glom your fly. They can get to be a terrible nuisance. I've never had it happen to me, mind you, but I've seen the time fish wouldn't give a friend of mine a minute's peace. They ate a serious chunk out of his fly-fishing time, just one glom after another."

"Geez, you mean the fish can actually get to be a real bother?"

"Oh, indeed they can, Vinnie. Over my many years of experience, however, I have managed to develop certain techniques to discourage fish from bothering my fly. But we can take up those advanced techniques at a later session."

Vinnie scratched his head and stared thoughtfully up at the ceiling. "So what's the point of fly-fishin' anyway if you can't keep and eat the fish?"

"The point? To fly-fishing? Well, it's uh . . . uh . . . the point is . . . Do you know anything about existentialism, Vinnie? No? Well, then, let's not get into the philosophy of absurdity at this point in your introduction to fly-fishing. Any other questions?"

"So how much is this gonna cost me? To get started fly-fishin'?"

"Is your home mortgaged?"

"No."

"Good. Car payments? Kids in college?"

"No. But you're startin' to scare me."

I told him I was only joking. "Really," I said, "all you'll need to get started are a dozen or so flies, some line and leader, a reel, and either a fishing pole or a fly rod."

"That don't sound too bad. What's the difference between a fishin' pole and a fly rod?"

"Abut three hundred dollars."

Vinnie swallowed hard. "Okay, I'll go with the fly rod."

"Good choice."

"How about flies?" Vinnie asked. "How much do they cost?"

"If you go down to the fly shop and buy them, you can pick up flies for about two dollars each."

"Geez, that seems kind of high for a bit of fluff and feathers tied to a hook. Maybe I should tie my own."

"You can certainly do that, Vinnie, in which case your flies shouldn't run you much more than fifty bucks each."

"How come?"

"Well, it's basically the principle your wife relies on when she chooses to buy a kitchen shelf for a hundred dollars instead of letting you build one for five."

"Oh, so Mavis told you, did she? Hey, how come you know Mavis, anyway?"

"I don't, Vinnie. Just calm down. It's simply a universal law. That's how I know Mavis is going to say, 'Are you crazy? You want to spend five hundred dollars for some dyed rabbit fur, a chicken skin, and a few tools!' And what are you going to reply, Vinnie? 'Yeah, it's for some flies that otherwise would cost me two bucks each.'"

"I get your point. Okay, I guess I'll just buy the flies. Anything else?"

"Actually, there are few other odds and ends."

"Like what?"

"Well, let's see, you'll need a fly-fishing vest. And, then, you really should pick up at least a couple extra rods of different weights. And a couple extra reels. And spare spools. Let's see, is there anything else? Oh, yeah, you'll also need assorted chest waders, hip boots, wading staff, wader-patching kit, float tube, fins, canoe, net, nine different lines, spare leaders, tippet material, leader and tippet holder, nymph indicators, dry fly floatant, line dressing, nippers, forceps, leader sink, lead, hook hone, identification kit, magnifying glass, thermometer, polarizing sunglasses, licenses, permits, fishing regs, briefcase in which to carry licenses, permits, and fishing regs, and—"

"Stop!" cried Vinnie. "I get the idea!"

"Once you're properly outfitted, of course," I continued, "you will have to start learning the Latin and common names, stages, and habits of about nine dozen insects, and—"

"Stop!" cried Vinnie again. "I can't stand it! This fly-fishin' is already stressin' me out and I haven't even started! I don't know how you stand it!"

"Well, like I said, Vinnie, you're just too old. You've got to start young, so you have time to develop the nerves of steel required for fly-fishing. It's not just anybody who can whip that bit of fluff and feathers out over a trout stream. You got to be tough."

Vinnie took out a handkerchief and wiped beads of sweat off his forehead. "Well, thanks, guy. I can see now I ain't cut out for it, that fly-fishin'. Just don't have the nerves."

"Well, don't feel bad, Vinnie," I said, patting him on the shoulder. "Many are called but few make it past the fly shop."

Poor devil. If I'm not mistaken, I detected some kind of harness under his jacket when I patted his shoulder. No doubt a corrective device for a work injury. So then I felt even worse for having been so hard on him. But, hey, you just can't knowingly let a guy take up fly-fishing with the idea that it's going to relieve his stress.

A Dimple in Time

The other day I lay flat on my back in the snow of a stubble field. I counted my toes as one by one they froze and fell off and rattled around inside my boots.

Alan Liere and Alan Knott lay on their backs in the snow not far away.

I could hear the distant cries of geese as they passed hundreds of yards to the east of us and hundreds of yards to the west of us.

"I like to put the decoys in a C formation," Alan L. said.

"I like them the way we have them," Alan K. said.

We continued to stare up at the empty sky directly above our horizontal canvas blinds. *What am I doing here*, I thought, *when I could be home in a cozy bed, perhaps arising to a hot breakfast of fresh-baked muffins and* . . . Then I thought of my grandmother.

Gram looked up from her fresh-baked muffins, rested her hands on her ample hips, and frowned at me. "I'll tell you why you don't catch more fish. It's because you have no patience.

It takes patience to catch fish. Now, your grandfather had patience. He'd go down to the crick and come back with a milk bucket full of the nicest trout you ever seen."

"Or maybe that's my problem," I blurted out. "All those milk buckets full of fish he brought back. There's none left for me."

"Don't sass! It's lack of patience, that's your problem."

Gram was right, of course. I do lack patience. I'll cast a couple of times into a hole, and if I don't get any takers I move on to the next one. My friend Vern Schulze will come along behind me and spend an hour at the first hole. He'll try a dozen different flies; five different sizes, change his leader, his hat, his casting technique, his name and address, and finally, sure enough, he will catch a fish. "Hey, Pat," he'll yell at me. "I caught a fish out of that hole you just left!" Actually, I will have fished the whole stream by then and be on my way back.

Vern has two sons, Jim and Wayne. Wayne is normal but Jim is patient. Jim makes his dad look like a person in a permanent frenzy. Years ago, when the trails weren't so steep and there was more oxygen in the mountain air, Vern and I would take the boys on hikes to high mountain lakes.

It is the nature of these lakes to suddenly "turn off," at which times days will sometimes go by before the fish will decide to feed again. Even now, a good fraction of a century later, I can see Jim as a boy of twelve perched immobile on a rock, staring relentlessly at a dimple his limp line makes in the water. He seemingly would sit there from sunup to sundown without twitching so much as a finger. Maybe he would even be there through the night and the next day, too; I can't remember. I would have felt sorry for him, except Jim always caught more fish than the rest of us put together. Patience seems so unfair.

My problem, I think, is that I think. I'm sitting out in a boat and haven't had a strike in hours. I think, *What am I* doing out here? *This is crazy! I might just as well be sitting in my living room holding a rod out over an empty fishbowl. And I'd have TV besides! How much time has passed? Three minutes? Is that all? Must be something wrong with this watch. And my back aches. I've never had a backache like this before. It's probably something serious, too. Could be fatal. If I weren't sitting out here in a boat staring at a dimple in the water I could have it checked by a doctor. Wonder how long I've been out here now. Four minutes! What is wrong with this stupid watch?*

Twenty years ago I picked up another friend, Dave Lisaius. He seemed normal enough at first. He enjoyed fishing and hunting and, even more, telling stories about fishing and hunting, many of which were true. Then one day we went fishing together. It was horrible! Of all the patient people I'd fished with over the years, Dave was the most patient. Whether or not a single fish had made its presence known, he would insist upon exhausting the very last bit of daylight before turning in.

"Well," I'd say, "I guess they're not biting today."

"They will," he'd reply, not looking up from the little dimple his line made in the water. "It's only a matter of time."

A matter of time. That is the mantra of the patient person. He will repeat it over and over. "They'll start feeding soon. It's only a matter of time."

Yes, but how much time? An hour, a day, a month, an infinity?

If I go an hour without a bite, I begin to suspect that all the fish have disappeared from the world. In another hour, I am certain of it. In another hour, I realize that fish have never existed in the first place.

I'm convinced that the very act of fishing is one of the first signs of serious dementia. It is giving in to the delusion that something called fish once actually occupied space in the world—Santa Claus, Easter Bunny, Tooth Fairy, fish.

"I CAN'T STAND THIS ANYMORE!" I once screamed at Dave.

He didn't move. He continued to stare at the dimple his line made in the water. "Eat a sandwich," he said.

I got out the pretzel sticks and used them to build an exact replica of Buckingham Palace. The light was now fading. "Give it up, Dave," I said. "They're never going to bite. Fish don't even exist."

He stared at the dimple. "There's time enough. I can still see my line."

The other day at lunch I told him, "You are absolutely the most patient person I know. And I have known some extremely patient persons."

"Thanks," he said.

"I didn't mean it as a compliment," I said.

"Between us, who catches the most fish?" he said.

"You do," I said. "What has that got to do with anything?"

"Well, the reason you don't catch more fish is that you have no patience."

I squinted at him. "You know, Dave, in just the right light you remind me a lot of my grandmother."

But at that moment I was lying on my back in the snow of a stubble field, waiting for the geese to come in to our decoys. Fat chance. And then the geese were there, clouds of them, and the two Alans and I were up shooting and yelling and feeling like twenty years old again and it was so exciting and invigorating! See, all it takes is a little patience.

Spare Me the Details

(What Are the Odds of a Double Flat?)

My rich friend **Fenton** Quagmire and I were discussing predicaments over coffee in Gert's Gas 'n' Grub the other day. I said my worst predicament was running out of gas far back in the mountains. Quagmire responded with a bitter and disdainful laugh.

"I suppose you have something you think is worse," I said.

"I do," he said, staring blankly out the rain-streaked window. He shuddered, as if the mere memory of the disaster were too much for the human nervous system to bear. "The horror of it!" he muttered, doing his best impression of Marlon Brando. "Oh, the *horror* of it!"

The elderly couple in the next booth got up, paid their bill, and fled. Gert rushed over to our table. "Are you two reminiscing again?" she demanded.

"Yeah," I said.

"Well, stop it! You're scaring the other customers!"

While waiting for Gert to settle back into the dreary depths of her eatery, I got the coffeepot off its little warmer and gave each of us our ninth refill. Such is the sorry state of eating establishments these days, it is almost impossible for a waitress to remember refills after the fifth or sixth one. Settling myself once again into our booth, I told Fenton to continue with his worst predicament.

For a long while he appeared to be absorbed in peeling up pieces of the table's disintegrating oilcloth. "All right," he said at last. "I guess I can tell you."

I will here give you Quagmire's account but without the groans and grimaces, which I find impossible to reproduce.

He was at the time a young and lowly executive in a Blight City corporation, a job he found to be personally suffocating. Thus did he spend every leisure moment in the pursuit of fishing and hunting, or at least in preparation to go fishing and hunting. One August afternoon he slipped away from his office and drove up one of the valleys that converge on our little town of Blight City. He had nothing more in mind, he said, than perhaps filling in a few spaces on his life list of birds actually spotted by himself, or possibly species spotted by friends of his, or even vague rumors of birds said to have passed through the valley at one time or another.

Birds seemingly being in short supply that day along the Blight River, he turned off on the road leading up along the west branch of the river. Although he didn't mention it, I am quite sure he involuntarily picked up speed while passing the Cut 'n' Run Bar, the last business establishment before the road begins to wind up toward Desolation Ridge. The bar prides itself on its evil reputation, which I think is vastly exaggerated, despite the disappearance of a few tourists.

"Don't tell me you drove up to Desolation Ridge!" I said. "It was the middle of summer!"

"I was scouting elk," Quagmire said. "Besides, I thought I

might even get to see a blue grouse. I haven't spotted one in years."

"Yeah," I said, "but the deer flies are thick up there in the summer. And if there isn't a strong enough breeze, the mosquitoes swarm up from the headwaters of Slippery Creek."

"All too true," he said sadly.

Continuing with his tale of misery, Quagmire explained that he was only about three miles from Desolation Ridge when he came to a tree across the road. He was driving his four-by-four pickup truck and he calculated that the truck would easily clear the top portion of the tree, which it did. Unfortunately, a sharp point of a broken branch pierced like a spear through the left front tire. With a *whoosh*, the tire instantly collapsed down onto its rim.

I should mention here that Quagmire was still wearing his business clothes, although he had removed his jacket and tie and hung them on the gun rack in the rear window. He soon discovered that because the truck had dropped all the way down onto the rim, there wasn't enough clearance to get the jack under the vehicle in the appropriate place. Therefore, he had to dig a hole under the truck using only his hands and some sharp sticks, which were in plentiful supply. Adding to the predicament, however, was the fact that the truck had also dropped onto the tree, a section of which had to be removed before he could start digging his hole with the sharp sticks and his hands.

Three hours later Quagmire had managed to remove a portion of the tree and could then begin to dig the hole. I am still unclear as to how he removed the section of tree, because he responded to my inquiry about it with only a wild-eyed look and his arms thrown in the air, as if that provided any useful information whatsoever. I do recall there was in his account some mention of a penknife. He then managed to scoop out a hole in the rocky, sunbaked surface of the road and in scarcely more than another hour was able to get the jack in place. The deflated tire was soon replaced with the spare.

Now he had no spare.

I can only assume that the trouble resulting from the flat tire caused Quagmire to drift into a momentary state of insanity. Any normal person who finds himself far up in the mountains without a spare will turn around at first opportunity and head toward civilization as quickly as possible.

"What are the odds," Quagmire said, his eyes brimming with tears, "that you will have two flats on the same trip into the mountains, particularly when you haven't had a flat tire in twenty years!"

In my opinion, the odds are much better than you might think. Quagmire's faulty reasoning was such, however, that because he had come this far, he certainly wasn't going to stop three miles short of Desolation Ridge. He drove on.

Standing on the ridge and taking in the spectacular view of half a dozen mountain ranges fading to the faintest blue in the far distance, Quagmire did not even mind the cloud of deer flies that had almost instantly detected fresh sustenance. Nor did he heed the ascending roar coming from the headwaters of Slippery Creek. What did catch his attention was a hissing sound. Hoping it would be nothing more than a rattlesnake at his feet, he turned and peered down at the front tire he had just changed. It was well on its way to becoming flat.

Had a psychologist been on hand, he would have had the opportunity to witness a mind in the act of becoming seriously unhinged. Quagmire immediately rushed the jack under the truck and removed the tire. He then put on his suit jacket, for evening was approaching, and began rolling the tire down the mountain and toward the nearest gas station, which was approximately thirty-five miles distant.

"Let me interrupt for a moment," I said. "At the very least, a rational person would have walked to the station without the tire, bought two new ones, had them mounted on appropriate wheels, and paid the station owner or one of his assistants an exorbitant price to drive him back up and replace the tire. Extricating yourself from a predicament is seldom cheap."

"Shut up," Quagmire said and continued with his tale.

While he was chasing his spare tire down one of the steeper grades of Monument Road, Quagmire was picked up by a burly woodcutter in a truck.

"So you got a ride right away," I said. "And you call that a predicament. Ha!"

"Yes, I call that a predicament! The guy turned out to be a poacher and a madman!"

The woodcutter said his name was Lud Grossbeak. When they had gone scarcely a mile, Lud spotted a ruffed grouse alongside the road.

"There's my supper," he said, removing a rifle from the rack behind the seat. "The nice thing about ruffed grouse is they're both stupid and delicious."

Realizing that grouse season was at least a month away and also that Fish and Game took a dim view of shooting grouse on roads, Quagmire blurted out, "Is that legal?"

"An eagle!" cried Lud, peering about. "Where's an eagle? I've always wanted a stuffed eagle!"

The grouse took advantage of this diversion to fly off into the woods.

"I guess it was a crow," Quagmire said, sheepishly, realizing that he was now in the company of a serious lawbreaker.

"You must be from the city," Grossbeak said, "to mistake a crow for an eagle."

"Yes, I am," Quagmire confessed. "From the city. I'm sorry I distracted you from getting your supper."

"Ah, that's all right," Grossbeak said. "There's lots of grouse on this road. Probably see another one before we're out of the mountains. Maybe even a deer."

Fortunately, they didn't see another grouse, or a deer, either, but in a short while they approached the Cut 'n' Run tavern. At that point, Lud said, "I hope you don't mind if I stop here for a moment. I have a score to settle with the jokers inside. When I stopped by this morning, they started funnin' me."

"Funnin' you?" Quagmire croaked.

"Yeah, pokin' fun at me. I was all by myself then and didn't have anybody to back me up."

"Back you up?" Quagmire said, his voice now scarcely more than a gravelly whisper.

"Yup. You just watch my back while I take care of business. You got your knife on you, don't you?"

"A penknife," Quagmire gasped. "A very dull penknife."

"A penknife!" Lud exclaimed. "Why, that won't do. On second thought, maybe you better slip over here to this side. You can be the getaway driver."

"Okay," Quagmire croaked. He slid over and took the steering wheel in a death grip. Lud went into the bar and a few minutes later came rushing out. He yelled, "Let's go!"

Quagmire let out the clutch and stomped on the gas. Then he hit the brake and let Grossbeak climb in.

When they got to town, Quagmire bought his rescuer and himself steak dinners, after which Lud wished him well and said he had to be on his way.

"So long, Lud," Quagmire called after him. "Thanks again for the ride."

"How come you called Boris 'Lud'?" the cashier asked.

"Boris?" Quagmire said.

"Yes, his name is Boris Minsk. He's a professor of abnormal psychology at the college. Most people claim he's a great practical joker, but Boris says he's really doing research."

All this time I had sat listening patiently to Quagmire's report on his ultimate predicament. "Ha!" I said. "And you call that a predicament! I ran out of gas on Mount Baldy and then had a nasty disagreement with a rowdy gang of bikers."

"Those guys usually aren't nearly as tough as they look."

"Oh, yeah? They had pedaled all the way to the top of Mount Baldy. Is that tough or what?"

"Well, I neglected to mention one small detail," Quagmire said. "I had left a beautiful young woman in the car up on Desolation Ridge."

"You win," I said.

"It was all innocent enough. She was an excellent photographer, and I figured if I did see a blue grouse, I'd have her along to take a picture of it."

"Right," I said.

"But that's not all. The only person I could call to drive me and my new tire back up to the ridge was Sue Ellen, my fiancée."

Fortunately, Quagmire had told the beautiful young woman to hide behind a bush whenever she heard a car coming up the mountain, because, he explained, his fiancée didn't understand much about photography. When Sue Ellen and he drove up to Quagmire's pickup, there was no sign of the girl, which was a great relief to him. But then Sue Ellen wanted to sit in the car and talk. She said she hated to tell Quagmire this but the engagement was off. She couldn't stand to be married to someone who got into the kind of predicaments he did. After half an hour or so she turned her car around and left.

"As I started to put the new tire on," Quagmire continued, "a cloud of deer flies and mosquitoes rushed out from behind a bush and tried to kill me with a rock. It was Blanche, of course, and—"

"Blanche!" I said. "Your first wife's name was Blanche!"

"Yeah, after what I had put her through, I felt the only decent thing was to marry her. What kind of predicament is that!"

The Haircut

I was out looking for a new barber. My last barber did a great job, but I teased her one day and she got mad. Never have your hair cut by somebody you've made mad. So I was out looking for a new barber.

My friend Wapshot told me I should go back to our old barber, Curly Higgens. Curly still charges eight dollars for a haircut. He has charged eight dollars for the last twenty years. For eight dollars he gives the basic old-fashioned haircut, with holes shaved out for the ears. He somehow achieves the bowl effect without the bowl. It's quite impressive. For sixteen dollars he gives you a shampoo and a styling. The styling looks exactly like the eight-dollar haircut. So all his customers wash their own hair and go for the eight-dollar cut.

I view getting my hair cut nowadays primarily as an irritation. Back when I was a boy, it was a major event. A haircut cost twenty-five cents. That was for kids. Maybe everybody's haircut cost twenty-five cents or maybe adults got theirs for only fifteen cents.

Getting a haircut was a major part of one's education back then. The men sat around and talked as if you weren't there, and you pretended to read old copies of *Look* or *Life* magazines and learned all kinds of things you weren't supposed to know. Once in a while someone would say, "Little pitchers have big ears." I never knew what that meant. After a while, though, the men would forget about little pitchers having big ears and would get back to topics that really interested them.

The barber and I never got along. Mostly it was because of the board. By the time I was seven, I thought the board was an insult and refused to sit on it. This, of course, upset the barber, as well as giving him a crick in the back from bending over to do his snipping. As I say, never make your barber mad.

My mother never cared one way or the other how my haircuts looked, as long as most of my hair was removed by the time she returned to pick me up. Kids didn't pay much attention to haircuts, either, except they would say to me, "Ha! You refused to sit on the board again, didn't you?" That's probably why I've had so much trouble with barbers. Maybe they share some kind of historic database: "This guy refused to sit on the board when he was seven years old."

The barbershop was a lovely place in the old days. It was full of smoke and stories. Men in mackinaws and hats and logging boots would be smoking cigars and cigarettes and pipes, and telling all kinds of outrageous lies. You, the little kid, were the only one who believed them, apparently, because at the end of the lie there would be a general roar of disbelief from the men. Still, if you listened carefully and remembered, you could pick up all kinds of good hunting and fishing tips, which you followed until you were twenty and realized they were all useless.

I finally decided to go to Curly, as Wapshot had recommended. Heck, eight dollars is eight dollars. I went on a Saturday, when the place was full, just as if most of the guys there actually worked during the week. They were all fishermen, and some of them came only for the talk. I suspect the talk was always good. But such lies! You can't believe the lies. It was just like the old days.

Finally, my turn at the chair came. Curly remembered me. "Got tired of those ritzy twenty-dollar cuts, did you?"

"I made Alice mad," I said. "So I'm back for the eight-dollar cut."

"Well, you make me mad, too," Curly sniffed.

"Yeah, but I can't tell the difference with you," I said.

"Al Finley was in the other day," Curly said.

"Figures," I said. "He's really cheap."

"True, but he told me what happened when he went fishing with you and Retch Sweeney."

"All lies," I said. "It never happened. What'd he say?"

The barbershop fell silent. Smiles were exchanged. At last assured that he had everyone's attention, Curly repeated the latest slander by Al Finley.

It seems Retch and I had taken Finley fishing up on Goose Creek. He was fishing upstream from us. Suddenly, the bank gave way and he plunged into the stream. He saw Retch and me racing toward him with a long driftwood pole we had snatched up. He thought we were going to use the pole to pull him back to shore. Instead, we used it to push him to the far side of the stream, away from the good holes we were fishing!

"What a liar!" I said, as the group expressed their amusement. "Finley was so busy blowing into that little red tube to inflate his inflatable vest, he had no idea what was going on. He was yelling 'Help, help' between puffs."

"You mean there was no pole?" Curly said.

"Of course not! What kind of monsters would use a pole to

push a drowning man to the other side of the stream, unless of course he was going to ruin some really good fishing."

"Finley said you let him go right over a waterfall."

"A waterfall! He wants to call that a waterfall, I suppose he can. Sheesh! Besides, we didn't let him go over it. He did it on his own, screeching like a banshee, I might add! He may have thought it was an actual waterfall he was coming to, but still, it's embarrassing to hear a grown man screech like that."

Curly continued with his report. "Then Finley said on the way home you and Retch bought some pigs and put them in the back of his new station wagon and the pigs got loose from their gunny sacks and made a terrible mess of the vehicle."

I shook my head. "Pigs! Where does Finley get this stuff, anyway?"

"And that's not all," Curly went on. "He said one time you and Retch made him sit under the hood of an old pickup truck and act as a human fuel pump while the truck backed up the side of a rocky gorge, and then you drove twenty miles to town through a blizzard without giving him a chance to get out from under the hood."

Well, that was too much. "A human fuel pump!" I said, rolling my eyes. "That Finley is such a liar. He would be pretty good, too, except he pushes the exaggeration way too far."

"Yeah, I thought it was pretty far-fetched, even for you," Curly said. He held a mirror to the back of my head. "Now, how does that look?"

I screeched like a banshee.

When I got home, my wife, Bun, took one look at my haircut and said, "What did you do now, make the barber mad again?"

"Eight bucks," I said.

"Looks good," she said.

"Any calls?"

"Only Retch. He said one of your pigs died."

"Darn! Just like a pig to pull something like that. By the way, Bun, you got a needle handy?"

"What do you need a needle for?"

"Oh, I got a sliver when Retch and I were fooling with a driftwood pole the other day. Which reminds me, you wouldn't believe the outrageous lies Al Finley is telling all over town."

"Try me," she said.

Bed-and-Breakfast

The white gravel driveway appeared to have been freshly washed and combed, and I wasn't at all sure it was meant to be driven on. Maybe it wasn't a driveway at all but one of those Japanese sand gardens, a work of art, really. It would be just like me to park on some guy's Oriental Picasso. I imagined my old truck squatting in the middle of it, belching exhaust and dripping oil, and a screaming Samurai gardener running out of the shrubbery with a six-foot-long hedge-lopper. The image didn't improve my mood.

I glanced uneasily at the house. Even if I couldn't quite put my finger on it, I sensed something sinister hovering over the place. It was all so, well, *orderly.*

"I don't like it," I said.

"Don't be silly," Al Finley said. "It's a perfectly lovely bed-and-breakfast."

Finley, one of my regular fishing partners, is a former banker, very precise (read "persnickety") about everything. It was easy to see why this place would suit him so well.

"It's too weird," I said. "This guy doesn't know us from Adam, but for a few bucks, actually quite a lot of bucks, he invites us to spend the night, turns part of his house over to us. He's gotta be crazy to do that. So right from the start we know we're sleeping in a house with a crazy person. He could be an ax murderer! Probably got gullible houseguests like us planted all over the property."

"Please!" whined Finley. "Just this once, pretend to be one of the species. It's a B and B, for pity's sake."

We got out and walked up a white gravel path to the house, the gravel crunching quietly under our feet. There really was something creepy about the whole place: the neatly trimmed grass, the excessively tidy flower beds, the immaculate walks, the pastel pink siding of the house, so tastefully contrasting with the blue trim. Or was it the row of precisely spaced pots of petunias along the porch railing? Someone had to have got out a tape measure to achieve that kind of spacing.

"I don't like it," I said. Everything is so . . . so . . . so tidy! It's unnatural. Gives me the creeps."

"Combing your hair gives you the creeps," Finley snapped. "Listen, I talked to young Mr. Jones on the phone and he seemed most pleasant, a very soft-spoken gentleman."

"Soft-spoken! That's the very worst kind, Finley! *Soft-spoken* has serial killer written all over it! Don't you ever watch *America's Most Wanted*? C'mon, let's get out of here, before it's too late."

"No way! We'd forfeit our very substantial deposit!"

Ignoring my pleas, Finley rapped the door's antique knocker. Edgar Allan Poe responded.

"Yesss?" Poe inquired. "What may I do for you gentlemen?"

Finley explained that we were to be paying houseguests for the next few days, while we fished the local lakes and streams.

Poe looked me up and down. "Indeed?" he said, as if recalculating in his head some silly mathematical error. "Well, come in, gentlemen. Oh, dear, and do remove your shoes. The carpets, you know."

"No problem." Finley started to sit down in a chair to untie his shoelaces.

"Oh, stop! Stop! Not in that chair!" cried out Poe. "Much too delicate for a man of your, er, stature. Perhaps you could just hop around on one foot while you untie your laces. By the way, I trust you brought ties and jackets, for lounging about in the living room with the other guests. I like to maintain at least a modicum of civility in this otherwise rather uncouth part of the world."

Finley gave me a pained look. I didn't know if it was because of the jackets and ties or because of his trying to keep his balance as he hopped up and down the hallway on one foot.

"Please notice," continued the proprietor, "that I have posted on the bathroom door a brief list of rules, fifteen to be exact."

"Fifteen rules for staying in your house?" I said.

"No, for using the bathroom. The house rules are posted elsewhere."

"That's fine," I said. "No problem there. And let me assure you, sir, that Winston will be no trouble. You won't hear so much as an 'arf' out of him."

"Arf?" said Poe.

Finley came to rest, one shoe on and one shoe off. Without missing a beat, he added, "Indeed, we have never had a single complaint regarding Winston."

"I'm sure you will agree, sir," I continued, "that such a record is remarkable, considering how many hotels, motels, and inns these days harbor a prejudice against dogs."

"Dawwwwgggs!" cried Poe. "You have a dawwwwg?"

"My goodness, yes," said Finley. "I'm sure I mentioned

Winston when I sent in the deposit, but perhaps I only assumed you would understand Winston was a dog. Winston loves to go fishing with us, and we can't bear to leave him at home. Oh, you would enjoy a chuckle if you ever saw Winston carry on when someone hooks a fish."

"You have a dawwwggg?"

"Oh, don't get the idea he still carries on like that," I said. "Old Winston, he's about seventeen now and a bit absent-minded, but he almost never fails to give a little yelp when heeding a call of nature. He's very good about that, you see, so you needn't worry about your carpets or anything like that. Sure, there may be the occasional small accident. Winston sometimes dreams he's already outside, standing next to a tree or a fireplug. But, hey, we're not the kind of guys to stick our host with any cleaning bills, no siree."

"You have a dawwwwggg?"

Ten minutes later we were back in the truck and headed out to another B and B that Poe had recommended as being more suited to us. Finley counted our deposit while I drove.

"The guy return it all?" I asked.

"Yeah," Finley said. "In fact, he was so relieved to get rid of us that he threw in an extra twenty."

"He should have thrown in an extra fifty, insulting Winston like that!"

"Yeah, that hurt. It would have hurt a whole lot worse, of course, if we had actually brought Winston along."

"And if Winston even existed."

Presently, we came to our second B and B, a large old house I will mercifully describe only as picturesque. It was, however, conveniently located on the shore of a lake we intended to fish. A little shack was perched on the far end of a somewhat dilapidated dock. A faded sign on the shack advertised, with appealing simplicity, BAIT.

"Wow!" I said. "This is my kind of place."

"Holy cripes!" cried Finley.

"Listen, Finley," I said, "I venture this is a B and B where we'll be able to kick back and relax with our shoes on and our ties and jackets off, without worrying about all the rules of some prissy owner. And speaking of owners, I do believe that lady approaching us at this very moment must be the proprietress."

It would be unkind of me to describe in any detail this rather striking lady, who had obviously left a good seventy years or more in her wake. I will confine my description, therefore, only to her slippers, in which she was at that very moment striding through a shallow but very muddy puddle. The slippers, at least pre-puddle, were pink and fuzzy, each adorned with two droopy protrusions that I guessed were, or once had been, bunny ears. Well, okay, I might also add that her thick tangle of gray hair was topped by a battered felt hat while the rest of her ensemble consisted of a faded work shirt and a pair of bib overalls that made no pretense of ever having made the acquaintance of soap and water. She gave Finley a big smile and a slap on the back, one or the other of which buckled his knees. Her gravelly voice greeted us lustily.

"Howdy, sports! I reckon you're up here to do some fishin'! Well, you come at the right time and to the right place! The fishin' is great and I'm all stocked up for a couple more guests."

"It sounds wonderful," I said.

"And I got crawlers galore," she added.

"I somehow surmised that," said Finley, peering wistfully back the way we had come.

"Just call me Tiffany," the lady said.

"Tiffany," said Finley.

"Yup," said Tiffany. "Now, ordinarily you'd be too late fer

dinner but we just finished up. So come on in and I'll slop some homemade chicken and noodles into a couple of bowls. Got some fresh bread to go along with it."

"Sounds perfect," I said.

"Tiffany," Finley said.

"Yup, Tiffany. By the way, we're all filled up, bein' it's this time of year when the fishin' is hot, so I hope you two fellas don't mind sharin' a bed."

"Not at all," I said.

"My worst nightmare," Finley said.

That night as we were about to drift off to sleep, Finley said, "I hope my rib cage isn't hurting your elbow."

"Not at all," I said.

"I have to apologize, Pat," Finley said. "Sleeping with you wasn't my worst nightmare."

"Thanks," I said.

"Happy dreams," Tiffany said. "I hope you fellas won't mind my snoring too much."

Lenny

October. Two more weeks. As was our habit each
morning, we Four Moscatoos met for coffee in the
company cafeteria. It was a sterile place, except for the food.
The decor was greenish plastic, some of it molded into tables
and chairs. The food was greenish plastic molded into roast
beef and chicken sandwiches and the plat du jour. There was
a rumor that someone had once eaten the plat du jour, but
that had never been confirmed.

"It's about time," Calvin said, sniffing a doughnut, then
placing it carefully back down on the table where he had found
it. Bob nudged the doughnut with his finger. We all watched
the doughnut for a moment, not simply because it was a point
of focus but to see if it did anything. It just sat there.

We were subversives. "This thing goes down Friday at seven
P.M. sharp," Bob said. "Synchronize your watches."

No one synchronized his watch. We knew, given past experience, it probably wouldn't go down before midnight on
Saturday.

"You getting your stuff together?" Calvin asked me.

"Everything but the ammo. I need more ammo."

"You can't have enough ammo," Rick said.

I nodded.

"He means *you* can't have enough ammo," Bob said. "The way you shoot, we'd have to carry a whole truckload of ammo."

"That's highly amusing," I said.

The Four Moscatoos consisted of Bob, Calvin, Rick, and me, warmed-over friends from college who had somehow converged on the same corporation. We were all single except for Rick, and he soon would be, his gorgeous wife at that very moment in the process of dumping him. The Q-Zed Corporation had us on the fast track for upper management because we were all young, tall, and had good hair, easy smiles, and entertaining palaver around the water cooler. What more could a CEO want in his VPs?

Certain persons above us in the corporate hierarchy had let it be known that the next opening for a management spot would be filled by one of the Moscatoos. The company, of course, didn't know there were Moscatoos. We were all for one and one for all and had formed a solemn pact that whoever went up first would pull the other Moscatoos along behind him.

"Shhh," Bob said suddenly. "Looks like we got company."

I glanced up. It was Pushkin. Lenny Pushkin was steering a straight course for our greenish plastic table.

Lenny clearly did not fit the Q-Zed executive mold. Indeed, he appeared to have been assembled in a chop shop from spare parts. Nothing seemed to fit. An overly large head perched atop a longish, knobby neck, which in turn connected to a gangly body. It was as if his designer had deliberately striven for a Halloween effect. His nose was large and his ears small. His eyes peered out from behind thick lenses that gave him a permanently startled look, the sort of thing that made you shoot a glance over your shoulder whenever you met him coming down a hallway. And he had bad hair, a frizzy reddish crescent that appeared to have been coiffed by a crazed gardener of no particular talent. Add to all this a slight stutter, not so much the result of a speech impediment but of lag time between his tongue and the blazing speed of his mind.

Lacking all the prerequisites for a Q-Zed vice president, Pushkin obviously posed no threat to the Four Moscatoos, and we generally enjoyed his company, if for no other reason than he raised the average IQ of the group by about thirty points. Most of all, Lenny knew how to do things. He was an excellent mechanic, for example. If you had car problems, which were endemic among the Moscatoos and their ratty old preowned sedans, Lenny was happy to come over and tune the zork, clean the whiffle, and adjust the kazoo. He was a handy guy to know.

"Pull up some plastic and rest your weary bones, Lenny," I said.

"What's up, Lenny?" Bob asked. "You look like the cat that swallowed the entire aviary."

Lenny was indeed beaming. "You're not going to believe this, guys, but you know the position that was opening up for a new vice president? Well, I got it!"

This announcement was followed by the dull sound of four Moscatoo jaws thumping a plastic tabletop.

"How? Why?" Calvin cried out. "I mean, congratulations, Lenny."

"Thanks," Lenny said. "Well, I guess it was because I did some algorithms for the dyna systems, which adjusted the parameters of the auto function and thereby increased profit by four hundred percent. Hey, this doughnut belong to anyone?"

"We saved it for you, Lenny," Rick said. "Bon appétit."

It was all so unfair. No one had ever even mentioned to us that Q-Zed regarded intelligence as a factor in promotion. It was yet another example of corporate deception.

"Hey, listen, guys," Lenny said. "I know you're all pretty disappointed one of you didn't get the promotion. But you're my friends, and I'm going to look out for you."

"What do you mean, look out for us, Lenny?" I asked.

"Why, I'm you're new boss, don't you know? I can take care of you guys. You're my friends."

The four of us mumbled a series of affirmatives: "Sure thing gosh yes good deal you got that right, old buddy."

"So tell me about the hunting trip," Lenny said.

"What hunting trip is that?" Bob said.

"The one you guys take every year the second half of October."

"Oh, that one," Rick said. "You know about the hunting trip, do you, Lenny?"

"Yes, I ran the numbers and deduced what you all were up to. Hey, don't get me wrong, I think it's great! It'll give us guys a chance to really get to know each other."

"Get to know each other?" Calvin said. "You want to go on the hunt with us, Lenny? It's all the way out to Wyoming, you know. Sleeping on the hard ground. Shaking rattlesnakes out of your sleeping bag. Fending off packs of coyotes. That sort of stuff. But you're sure welcome to come, Lenny."

"It sounds wonderful!"

"And burned food cooked over buffalo chips that looks and smells like buffalo chips and sometimes actually is buffalo chips."

"I love it! It's such a guy thing! You'll have me so stirred up I'll want to leave this very minute!"

"Gut piles! Horse dung!"

"You're giving me the warm shivers, guys! Gut piles! Horse dung! Poetry for the nose!"

Lenny joined us on the hunt for the next three years. He loved it. And he was tremendously useful, too. Not only did he fix our old sedans when they broke down, he was able to figure out the lights on our utility trailers. He even rigged up a system with a gas generator and batteries so we could have electric lights, a refrigerator, and, ultimately, a TV, so that we didn't have to spend two whole weeks cut off from news of wars, poverty, murders, and the collapsing economy. It was so disgusting—television on a hunting trip!

Furthermore, Lenny had consumed every known book on hunting and lectured us constantly on the finer and most arcane points of the sport. His knowledge of sporting firearms expanded miles beyond our comprehension. Soon he had mastered the mysteries of ballistics, muzzle velocities, and like that. It was so impossibly dreadful. All we wanted on our hunt was a modest amount of misery, a dozen or so nights around the campfire, a trophy or two, and a little venison.

Not only had Pushkin taken all the misery out of our hunting trip, he had taken all the fun out of it, too. But there was no way to get rid of him. He was, after all, our boss. Besides that, we couldn't stand to hurt his feelings, because at heart Lenny was a really nice guy.

"It's no fun anymore," Bob said one day while Lenny was out bagging yet another trophy. "Remember the great times we used to have, hunkered around the gas pump over at Higgens' Last Stop Station, while Leroy repaired the car in his little garage and we drank warm Orange Crush and ate peanuts and told stories with the cowboys who dropped by? That's all gone. It's history. Now we got Lenny not only overhauling our cars but cooking us eight-course French cuisine and playing us opera on the stereo. Besides that, he shoots all the best trophies."

"I sure hate to give up the hunt, though," Rick said. "My Ginger loves the hunt, too. Gives her time with her girlfriends."

"Yeah, Rick, you and Ginger make the perfect couple," I said. "Let's see now, how long's it been since Joan dumped you?"

"Three years."

"On what grounds was it?"

"The usual. Gross, inane, inattentive, boorish, dull, ignorant. Oh, yeah, and then there was that major incompatibility."

"Joan was a beauty, though."

"Beauty, heck, she was gorgeous," Bob said.

"Brilliant, too," Calvin said. "Loved French cooking and opera."

"She get married again?"

"Naw," Rick said. "Where's she going to find anyone good enough for her?"

We sat there in silence for a while, deep in thought.

The following October the Four Moscatoos were back to sleeping on the hard ground, eating burned beans, burned bacon, and possibly burned buffalo chips, and the nearest TV was sixty miles away in Casper. Lenny was gone. It was all good.

One night while we were sitting around the fire and listening to the mad ravings of the local coyotes, Calvin asked, "So, Rick, how long is it that Lenny and Joan have been married now?"

"Going on three months," Rick said. "Happy as larks, too."

"Joan's the perfect wife for Lenny," Bob said. "She goes for character and intelligence over good looks, loves French cooking and opera and most of the same things he does—a marriage made in heaven!"

"More like a marriage made in Wyoming," Rick said.

We all laughed.

"She does have that one bad drawback, though," Rick went on.

"Tell me again," Calvin said. "I love hearing it."

"She's vehemently opposed to hunting!"

"Hey," I said. "Don't knock it."

The Winter of Eighteen Months

When I was in first grade, the winter lasted eighteen months. Winters don't last that long anymore, but they did back then.

I attended first grade in a one-room, log-walled schoolhouse. My mother was the teacher. She earned seventy-eight dollars a month to teach all eight grades, serve as janitor, split and carry in the firewood for the old barrel stove to heat the school, and, at noon, cook the hot lunch. The neighbors envied us for being rich and enjoying such a luxurious lifestyle.

We lived in the schoolhouse. It didn't do me any good to stay home sick with the flu because I'd still be at school. So I never bothered to get sick. Or maybe the reason I didn't get sick is that every morning my mother would force me to drink a large spoonful of cod-liver oil, to keep me from getting scurvy, she said. We lived so far back in the woods we had no access to fresh fruits and vegetables, and so scurvy, presumably, was always a threat. Or maybe, as I thought at the time, Mom was just being mean. Cod-liver oil pretty much ruined life for me. I would have much preferred scurvy, whatever that is, to cod-liver oil.

Quite often today I receive letters from old men who try to compare their hardships as kids to mine. Some of their hardships were horrible. Unless they're lying. (Old men tend to lie a lot.) Not one of them, though, has ever mentioned cod-liver oil. So I win hands down.

Something school administrators of today might find impossible to believe is that the school got its drinking water out of nearby Goose Creek. A rope was attached to the bucket handle and then the bucket was hurled out into the middle of the creek and hauled back full of water. Maybe the idea behind hurling it out into the middle of the creek was that the water out in the middle was pure and the water along the bank wasn't. Or maybe it was that you couldn't see what was in the water in the middle of the creek. Nowadays, nobody drinks from creeks, for fear of catching dysentery, giardiasis, or something, but back then creek water was the least of our worries.

I learned to read that year, the year of the eighteen-month winter. It wasn't that I wanted to learn how to read. Sheer boredom forced me into it. I don't know much about educational theory, but I think maybe teachers should try boredom on their pupils. You would put a kid in a room with nothing but four bare walls. After a while, you would toss in a book. Any book would do, say, the volume A–B from a set of encyclopedias. He or she would snatch it up and learn to read in no time.

Anyhow, that's how we lived back then, when winter lasted eighteen months. I know how many months it lasted because I counted them. True, I've never been very good at math, but I'm pretty sure eighteen months is right.

All through September and October I hoped for snow. By November, there was no hope left in me. Then one day a single flake came drifting down. And then another. And another. "Yay!" I cheered. The snow kept coming and coming and coming, and pretty soon it was piled up higher than the schoolhouse windows. It was lovely.

Years later, after we had moved back near town, all that snow would have kept us home from school. But nothing keeps you home from school when you live in the schoolhouse. That was a major downside to my life back then, but at first I didn't care. I loved the snow.

Directly in front of the schoolhouse was a long, steep hill. Once as an adult I went back to the site. The Forest Service, which has no sense of history, had long ago burned down the school. I was saddened to see that my sledding hill had diminished also. It had turned into a rather pitiful thing, as hills go. I could scarcely imagine that I had swooshed down that gradual slope a thousand times as a six-year-old, my screams of elation muffled by my heart leaping into my mouth.

I remember one ride down the hill in particular. There was another first-grader, a little girl named Barbara. She was cute and smart and, typically, would have nothing to do with me. But one day I was hauling my sled up the long, steep hill, and Barbara came up alongside me and asked if she could ride down on the sled behind me. Suavely, I said, "Yep." Away we went, sizzling down the hill. I remember that Barbara had her arms wrapped tightly around me. You don't forget something like that, a cute girl wrapping her arms tightly around you. But it happened only that once.

For some reason, I began to lose control of the steering apparatus on the sled, if it had a steering apparatus. Then I noticed that we were headed directly for one of the posts that held up a small roof over the door of the school. I have a distinct recollection of my own desperation and helplessness at that moment, but I'm sure that Barbara, totally unaware of the approaching collision, felt nothing but the giddy excitement of the sled ride. Preparing for the worst, I reached down and got a good grip on each side of the sled. I can't recall if I shouted any warning to Barbara. I probably did not.

Whomp! We hit the post. I remained seated on the sled but the little girl flew over the top of me and bonked her head on the post. She bounced back down behind me.

Realizing that I had just killed Barbara, I immediately walked into the school and sat down at my desk, no doubt taking out a piece of paper and some crayons with which to color until the body was discovered. What impresses me to this day is that even at that young age I had the natural instincts of a criminal. If I had taken up that profession, I probably would have done quite well at it.

Presently, Barbara staggered into the schoolroom and sat down at her desk. She never again wrapped her arms tightly around me. In fact, I don't recall that she ever even spoke to me again. Such are the disappointments of youth.

Along about the twelfth month of winter, I began to tire of it. The sledding hill had lost all of its appeal. A whole army of bored snowmen occupied the school yard. Some of them were quite indecent. I don't know who made them that way. My igloo had lost much of its original glory. The snow fort had fallen into ruin. There was nothing left for me to do but stand in the schoolroom and stare out the window at the hideous snow.

I think it was during the seventeenth month of winter that I noticed bare ground beginning to appear around the trunks of trees. Gradually the snow retreated and pretty soon the sledding hill itself was bare. Tiny sprouts of green grass began showing up here and there. The snowmen, their eyes wide with terror, melted into icy pools. (If I had a bit more time and space, I'd explain how to make snowmen's eyes wide with terror.)

The Winter of Eighteen Months

It was then that my mother decided we could risk a drive into the roaring metropolis of Priest River, located about five hundred miles from the Goose Creek School. Nowadays, Priest River is only a nice little town about thirty miles from the site of the school, but back then it was a roaring metropolis and a long way off.

On the trip into Priest River, one of our tires went flat. While my mother and sister were changing it, I wandered off into the woods. There, amid some lingering patches of snow, I spotted a beautiful white flower, a trillium. I picked it.

But it was yet only the seventeenth month of winter. While we were still in Priest River, it began to snow. I had been tricked! On our way back to the school, a blizzard howled about the car and beat against the flailing windshield wipers.

I reached into my shirt pocket and pulled out the trillium. It was shriveled and faded. I began to cry.

"What on earth is the matter now!" Mom demanded. She never cried herself and was not fond of such displays in others.

"My flower died!" I howled.

Actually, I think my mother was rather pleased at my sensitivity, her son never before having shown any indication of that attribute. Years later she would smile and even laugh when she told the story about how I had once cried over the death of a flower.

What she never understood was, I wasn't crying over the death of a stupid flower. I was crying over the death of spring.

Christmas Goose

Everyone said my mother possessed an excess of goodness, although few ever realized the overflow generally got sloughed off onto me. "Mr. Farnsworth just got out of the hospital," she'd say. "So I want you to take this casserole over to his wife, and while you're at it you might as well shovel the widow Swartz's driveway. Oh, and on your way home split some firewood for old Mr. Johnson; a cord or two will do fine."

Dealing with my mother's overflow of goodness did wonders for my reputation. "He's such a good boy," Mom's friends would say. The gang of local toughs had about the same idea of me. "There's Goody Two-Shoes!" they'd yell. "Get him!"

Sometimes I'd have to yell to Mrs. Farnsworth and tell her to stand out by the sidewalk so I could hand off the casserole on my next time around, if I had enough lead on the gang. She'd complain to my mother that the casserole was cold and congealed when I finally got it to her. Then Mom would rant at me for an hour or so. "Here I make a nice casserole but you can't manage to deliver it while it's still hot! No, it's more important that you be out horsing around with the boys! Well, let me tell you, young man . . . !" Mothers and sons live in entirely different worlds.

Scarcely had Christmas vacation begun my junior year of high school than my mother had already run me ragged with the excess of her good deeds. One evening as I slumped exhausted in my chair at supper, Mom casually mentioned that Rancid Crabtree had stopped by earlier in the day. Rancid was an odorous old woodsman who resided in a shack back against the mountains behind town and more or less lived off the land, mostly hunting, fishing, and trapping. Oh, sure, he also kept a sharp eye out for the occasional odd job, just in case it might sneak up on him.

"I was so pleased he stopped by," Mom said, "because that gave me a chance to load him down with some preserves and a couple loaves of bread and a bag of apples. He must have visited for nearly an hour."

I sniffed the air. "I can tell," I said.

"Don't be such a smart aleck," Mom scolded. "You can't smell a thing, because I've had the windows open all afternoon. Nearly froze to death. Now, what was that he asked? Oh, yes, he wants you to go perch fishing with him at Blue Lake tomorrow."

I couldn't help but chuckle at such foolishness. "Rance just wants me to row the boat. No way!"

"I told him you'd meet him at the dock at eight. I don't want that old man out on the lake all alone. You'll do this little favor for me, won't you, dear?"

The time had finally come for me to put my foot down and stop this nonsense. "Absolutely not," I said. "Crabtree wants to go fishing, he can go by himself. And that's all I want to hear about it!"

I'm sure Rancid expected me to be waiting for him the next morning when his truck came rattling up to the Blue Lake dock.

"About time," I said as he trudged down to the boat carrying his fishing rod and a little tackle box in one hand and a bundle in the other. The bundle, wrapped in a piece of canvas tarp, looked to me like a bedroll.

"Hey, what's with the bundle?" I said. "We going fishing or camping?"

"Wahl, Ah'll tell you one thang, smarty-pants. Anybody what goes out with the likes of you ought to have the sense God gave a gnat to be prepared fer a catastrophe. 'Cause thet's what happens with you more often than not." He nodded at the bundle. "This hyars maw emergency kit."

As he stiffly stowed his bundle in the bow of the boat, I noticed that he increasingly had come to resemble a human question mark. *Geez*, I thought, *in another fifty years that could be me, all bent over, grizzled, and wrinkled, with hair growing out of my nose and ears and…*

"Gol-dang it!" Rancid snapped. "Would you stop sittin' thar starin' at me with yer mouth ajar and give this stove-up old man a hand into the boat, jist as if you was a civilized human bean!"

"Sorry, Rance," I said, helping him get settled in the bow seat. As we moved out into the lake, flock after flock of geese and ducks exploded into the air ahead of us, circled around, and came in to land behind, loudly expressing their indignation at having been disturbed.

"They sure do like hiding out in this Blue Lake Game Presarve," Rancid said. "The cowards. Ah tried to shoot me a Christmas goose out of maw pit but the beggars won't venture outta the presarve till it's too dark to shoot."

"Yeah," I said. "The beggars."

"They's in cahoots with the dang game department," he growled. "With Sneed in particular."

Rancid and the game department had been at odds for many years, mostly over Rancid's errors in arithmetic. As far as Rancid was concerned, the local game warden had his idea of limits and Rancid had his. Blight County's legendary game warden, Darcy Sneed, possessed the mythical talent of somehow being able to sense game violations miles apart in the county and then to show up simultaneously at each of those sites. Some people actually believed that. I was one of them. Sneed scared me to death. Naturally, there were the usual skeptical people who scoffed at Sneed's so-called mythical powers. They claimed he had to be either twins or triplets.

Rancid and I soon had a dozen or so perch in the boat and the old man said he figured we'd caught his limit for the day. I was glad to hear that, because dark clouds were rolling up over the mountains and the wind had increased its chill.

"Looks like a bad snowstorm might be rolling in," I said.

"Yep," Rancid said, smiling his snaggle-toothed smile. We were both pleased.

"Might be a white Christmas after all," I said. The ducks and geese seemed to agree with that assessment, because they started lifting off in great cacophonous masses.

"Patrick, my boy, row over toward that fer bank thar."

"What for?"

"Why, to get us outta the wind, thet's what fer. Shucks, might as well row us right into the middle of them cattails, give us a good windbreak."

I hauled on the oars for a few minutes. "How's that?" I said, indicating the wall of cattails rising well over our heads.

"Perfect," he said. "By the way, you know what Ah'd like fer maw Christmas dinner?"

"No, what?"

"A nice fat goose! Yessir, a goose!"

"A little late for that," I said.

"Yep," he said sadly. "See, what Ah does with a goose, Ah stuffs it with apples and oranges and onions and maybe some sweet taters, and then Ah lays some strips of home-smoked bacon across the breast, and shakes salt and pepper all over it, lots of pepper, and then Ah stick it in a real hot oven. You know how to check an oven to see if it's hot enough for a goose? Wahl, you stick your arm in the oven and if the oven's hot enough it'll curl yer arm ha'rs up. Little cookin' tip fer ya. Ah slides the goose in maw oven and roasts it till the skin turns all brown and crackly and greasy and the juices start to ooze out and every fifteen minutes or so Ah opens the oven and spoons the grease back over maw goose, 'cause grease is the secret to cookin' a goose . . ." And on and on he went until my mouth watered so it was almost leaking onto my shirt.

And then suddenly I heard some geese coming in low and fast and right toward us, heading flat-out for Texas. And Rance heard them, too. In one sudden smooth twisting motion, the old man snapped straight up off the bow seat, snaked his twelve-gauge pump shotgun out of his bundle, and whipped it to his shoulder.

"NOOOOOO!" I screeched. "YOU CAN'T SHOOT HERE . . ."

BLAM!

". . . IT'S A . . . game preserve."

A huge honker crashed stone-dead into the water not ten feet from the boat.

"You'll go to jail for this, Rance!" I shouted at him.

"Jail, nothin'! Sneed catches me one more time this y'ar, thet cranky old Judge Hogan'll give me the 'lectric chair! Uh, you ain't gonna squeal on me, are ya?"

It took me at least a minute to make up my mind. Then I

shook my head. The old reprobate knew I couldn't give him up. I couldn't let him go to jail, particularly over Christmas. I personally abhorred poaching and those who did it, but I knew now that unless I aided and abetted the criminal, he'd be spending Christmas in jail. It was wrong to help a poacher, and I knew it was wrong, but I was going to do it anyway. If we got caught, then we'd both be spending Christmas in jail. And for what? One measly goose. It suddenly occurred to me that I had never liked goose anyway, and now I liked it a whole lot less. "Well," I said to my fellow criminal, "how are we going to sneak this goose back to your shack without getting caught by Sneed?"

"Heh-heh," cackled Rancid. "Maw foolproof plan, thet's what. We drop the goose off at my secret spot up the lake here and tonight I'll sneak back and get it. Ain't nobody but me knows maw secret spot."

When we got to the secret spot, Sneed was already there, leaning against a tree while he cleaned his fingernails with a pocketknife. He never even bothered to look up.

"Fancy meeting you here, Crabtree," he said.

"And a fortunate thang it is, too, Sneed," Rancid responded. "'Cause we got a goose here made a terrible crash landin' and maybe broke its neck and so we's rushin' it to the vet and . . . Oh, no, Ah thank it jist expired. Well, if thet ain't the saddest thang Ah ever . . ."

One thing about Sneed, he always treated those he arrested with the greatest of courtesy. You almost thought he was doing you a favor, and you wondered if maybe you shouldn't thank him for going to the trouble of hauling you off to jail.

Cranky old Judge Hogan did send Rancid to jail. He told him the next time he was brought in for poaching it was going to be either hanging, the electric chair, or the firing squad, and maybe all three. Sneed spoke on my behalf, his argument being that I was probably too young and stupid to know any better than to hang out with an old rascal like Crabtree. The judge agreed, and let me off with a pretty mean scolding for assisting in the crime.

Of course it wasn't long before word got around that I'd been arrested for poaching. Naturally, my mother was furious and accelerated her excessive good works to the maximum, in the hope of someday restoring the family's reputation, such as it had been. One nice thing did come out of the catastrophe, though, and that was that our local gang of toughs thought it pretty darn neat that I'd been arrested for poaching. From then on they treated me just like one of their own—a fellow thug. On the other hand, all the old ladies and gentlemen to whom I delivered treats would stick their noses in the air and snort in disgust every time they saw me. They didn't think of me as such a good boy anymore, but at least they were too old to chase me around the block.

Mom didn't take Christmas Day off from her good deeds. "I baked dessert for that miserable old rascal Crabtree and his fellow criminals down at the jail," she told me. "So you take these pies down there before their dinner's over. Even poachers like Rancid and yourself deserve a dessert on Christmas."

Maggie Custer, the jail matron, wouldn't let me take the pies back to where the cells were but said she'd deliver them later. She said a big table had been set up in the exercise room and dinner was being served there. "They even got guests," she said.

"Guests?" I said. "Who?"

"Those miserable old bachelors Judge Hogan and Darcy Sneed, that's who!"

"Weird," I said. "What are they having?"

"Goose!"

"Goose?"

"Yeah, the very one old Crabtree poached. I guess after he got sentenced, Rancid started describing how he had planned to cook his goose, and pretty soon the judge and game warden were practically drooling on their neckties. So the judge said as part of his sentence Rancid would have to cook the goose! And Rancid did, but I guess the crazy old fool never heard of a temperature gauge. Stuck his arm in the oven to check the heat and hopped around here for fifteen minutes, screeching like a banshee! Burned all the hair off his arm, too."

Walking home I was pleased despite myself that Rancid had got his Christmas goose after all. But that's when I suddenly remembered that Rancid heated his shack with an old barrel stove. He didn't even have an oven! Heck, even if he had got away with poaching, how did the crazy old fool expect to roast a goose anyway?

Peak Experience

Several years ago, I read a book by a famous psychologist about peak experiences. Actually, I got only halfway through the first chapter and so never found out what the author meant by "peak experiences." I liked the term so much, though, that I have gone ahead and invented my own meaning, which is simply that in each person's various activities at one time or another he or she peaks out—has a peak experience. I know what you're thinking: some of your peaks aren't all that high. Listen, I'm not talking Matterhorns here. I simply mean The Best You've Ever Had.

Sometimes you don't even know you're having a peak experience when you're having it. You just think, *Hey, this ain't bad.* But then someday when you get to be old and crotchety you look back meditatively and say, *Holy cow! That was the best I ever had!* Occasionally, however, right in the middle of the peak experience itself, you know you're peaking out, and you say to yourself, *Wow, this is the one, man! It ain't never gonna get better than this!*

What I'm leading up to here, of course, is my own peak experience in the activity of fishing. (Sorry.) It happened a couple of months ago. Up until then, my peak fishing experience had occurred when I was a kid.

One day when I was about ten years old we had some kind of crisis at home. As I recall, we were expecting one of my mom's visiting rich cousins for dinner. Our cash being in somewhat short supply, like, nonexistent, Mom was seriously concerned about what to serve our guest for supper that evening. Her only option seemed to be gruel, which is sort of a watery substance with ambitions to be either soup or mush. So I piped up and said, "Don't worry, Mom, I'll go catch us some fish!"

Right away she brightened up. "Don't make me laugh," she said.

True, my fishing hadn't been so hot lately. Almost every morning I'd head down to the creek and return in the evening with only a couple of seven-inchers and maybe some small ones. Through some miracle that day, I returned home with two huge brook trout, each of them measuring more than twenty-two inches. In my fishing world, these were whales. My mother almost burst into tears when she saw them.

I didn't know at the time that this was a peak experience. But it was. In fact, it would be my peak fishing experience for the next fifty years. Even though I would later catch much bigger and more exotic fish, none of them ever measured up to those two brookies as a peak experience.

So about a month ago, my friend Al Liere called up and told me he had just heard from Michelle Peters, executive director of the Hells Canyon Visitors Bureau in Clarkston, Washington. Michelle had received an invitation for Al and me to fish for steelhead in Hells Canyon. This was strange. Both Al and I are pretty well-known in outdoor circles, particularly in the Pacific Northwest. Being aware of our reputations, a person would have to be crazy to invite both of us on the same trip. It made me nervous.

"You think it's safe?" I asked. "I mean, the guy doesn't show signs of violent tendencies or like that?"

"No, Victor's great and he's got a fantastic lodge just outside of Asotin, Washington, right on the Snake River. Sure, Victor knows I'm weird, but he hasn't even heard of you. He thinks you'll be normal and probably offset me. Ha!"

"Well, all right, then!"

Al is a humor writer. You never want to go anywhere with a humor writer. They're dangerous. They make their living writing about all their bad experiences. Al has so many disasters he can write for a dozen different magazines at the same time and never even begin to run out of material.

Here's the strange thing: Al is just as worried about going out with me as I am about going out with him. I don't know why. Still, we normally have a great time, weird though it might be. Our drive down to Hells Canyon was no exception. We soon got to telling some of the old stories and laughing ourselves giddy. At one point I said, "Al, remember the time at that writers' conference when you set fire to your pants, and Paul Quinnett said to those women, 'No cause for alarm, ladies, he's a humor writer!' And they seemed instantly to understand! Well, I was just thinking—"

Al interrupted. "Hey, wait a second! I don't remember seeing those funny-looking haystacks on our last trip down here. You remember them, Pat?"

"Can't say I do. They look as if they might be the work of space aliens."

"Yeah, that's what I thought."

"Got any idea where we are, Al?"

"Nope. There's a hitchhiker up ahead. He probably knows the way. Maybe we should give him a lift."

"Don't stop, Al!" I shouted. "Don't stop! It's Rod Serling!"

I just made that up. The guy only looked like Rod Serling. But it's the sort of thing we run into. Weird stuff. And maybe we really were in the Twilight Zone. Otherwise, how could we explain why our three-hour trip took seven hours. Spooky.

We eventually arrived at Victor and Dawna's Hells Canyon Resort and Fishing Guide Service. Victor and Dawna pulled out all the stops for us, with a cocktail hour, gourmet dinner, live performances by a cast of three, and finally a round of karaoke, during which I brought down the house with my rendition of "A Kiss to Build a Dream On." Oh, all right, I *emptied* the house, but that was okay. It was already way past my bedtime.

The Dalostos, Victor and Dawna, had shown us a great time, all right, but the real test would be the fishing.

"Don't worry about that," Victor said the next morning. "You'll catch steelhead, Pat, I can promise you that."

I couldn't help but smile. Al, on the other hand, burst out laughing, which I thought a bit excessive.

For the past thirty years, as Al knew, I'd been able to defeat every guide who was foolish enough to make that boast. Of my total fishing time over the years, I'd probably spent a couple of hundred hours fishing for steelhead. During that time, I caught a total of . . . Well, nobody's interested in hearing me boast about how many steelhead I caught while icing over day after day after day in a twisting, turning, back-wrenching drift boat and my hands turning raw and cracked and swollen and those stinking steelhead never . . . ! But, as I say, nobody's interested in hearing me boast about all the steelhead I've caught. So I won't.

The next morning we started off up the Snake River headed for Hells Canyon in Victor's twenty-eight-foot Bentz boat powered by two 320-hp jet motors. It seemed adequate. Something was eerily wrong, though. Both Al and I sensed it. The weather was beautiful, the boat performed superbly, and the crew was great. You have to pick up on omens like that.

And then it happened. Al made a couple of casts and right off hooked and landed a seventeen-pound steelhead. I hate that in a person. For my part, I'd made half a dozen casts but hadn't yet got my line in water. It was Victor's fault. He had equipped the rods with these high-tech reels that required dexterity and reflexes. Figures. There was this trigger you were supposed to squeeze and release, and then the reel did the rest. What kind of madness is that?

On my first cast, I fired the lure and a wad of salmon eggs like a bullet—straight back behind me! Somehow I managed to slam on the brake and stop the lure cold, but the wad of salmon eggs sizzled on, almost smacking Jeff Pyle, the resort manager, right between the eyes. And I didn't even know him all that well.

My next cast landed thirty feet up on the rocks but at least on the right side of the river, which was clearly a plus. And so it went. Because Dawna rebaited my hook after every attempted cast, I was going through bait like there was no tomorrow.

Finally, I had a major breakthrough—I got the hook in the water. While I was still savoring the round of applause, we came to the Imnaha Rapids.

I've never been much good at rating rapids as to number 3, number 4, etc. Back in our white-water canoeing days, my partner Retch Sweeney would shout out, *"Holy* [bleep]*!"* whenever we rounded a bend and sighted some particularly difficult rapids in our way. The number of letters in the bleep increased according to the degree of difficulty. Had Retch and I headed into the Imnaha in a canoe, I suspect the number of letters would have approached the upper teens. Just to disabuse the reader of any notion that I'm exaggerating the Imnaha, I will mention that early in the previous century it once sucked down a paddlewheel steamboat!

Victor jetted us up through the rapids as if they were nothing more than a Disneyland ride—well, sure, one of those rides where people scream their lungs inside out, but basically a lot of fun.

Just above the rapids we came to a deep pool about half a mile long, and Victor began making drifts the length of it, pointing out places for me to cast, then ducking, then taking the boat back up for another drift. By now, Al had caught and released a couple more steelhead, just as if he had nothing better to do. For my part, I mostly admired the spectacular scenery. Even though I had viewed the scenery of Hells Canyon several times before, I think a person—a sensitive and appreciative person like myself—can never get enough of the rock walls soaring up a thousand feet from each side of the mighty Snake River, the water flowing like a great endless deep-green ribbon of satin over . . . My lure caught on a rock. I gave an annoyed jerk to break it loose. The rock moved upstream.

I had a steelhead on! I had this big baby on for good, too! Wait! No! It turned and started streaking back downstream! Noooo! Everybody started screaming, "Don't let it get into the rapids! Don't let it get into the rapids!"

Despite this advice, I couldn't keep the fish from inching its way toward the rapids. And then it was in them. I was now fighting not only the steelhead but the whole Snake River as well! No way could I hold the steelhead against the power of the Imnaha. Then Victor yelled out, "Everybody hang on! I'm gonna back down through the rapids!"

"*Holy* [bleeeeeeep]*!*"

And then we were in the rapids tossing this way and that, the fish and I battling like crazy, the waves splashing up over the stern and soaking my pants, somebody—I think it was Dawna—holding me by the back of my belt to keep the fish, this big monstrous steelhead, from pulling me over the stern. My arms began to ache from the pressure of the rod, and I knew either the steelhead or my wrists would have to give out soon.

Suddenly, scarcely a year later, we slipped out of the roaring rapids into a deep and tranquil pool. And I still had the fish on! It gradually and grudgingly surrendered. Jeff slipped the net under the defeated steelhead and for a few seconds held it there, long enough for some photos to be snapped and for me to estimate that my fish was much bigger than any of Al's. (Al argued that one of his fish was longer and weighed more than mine. Sure, if you want to count inches and pounds.) Jeff lowered the net. As I watched that big silvery steelhead drift away into the green depths of Hells Canyon, I knew that my fishing had just achieved peak experience. Sorry, ten-year-old Pat, but those two brookies of half a century ago just don't cut it anymore. Victor directed me to two more big steelhead during the day, and they were fun, too, but once you've fought a fish all the way through the Imnaha Rapids, your other fishing can be high above the tree line but still a long way from the peak.

Driving home that evening, Al and I couldn't get over the fact that we had finally managed to go on an outing together, have a fantastic time, and still not get overtaken by disaster. It had all been just so perfect.

"Too perfect," Al said. "Say, that looks like a nasty storm

blowing in up ahead. Maybe we should spend the night in a motel. Got any idea where we are?"

"Nope," I said. "But there's a motel sign up ahead. Let's stop there."

"Sounds good to me! I could use a nice hot shower."

Norman, the guy at the motel desk, bore an uncanny resemblance to Tony Perkins. At the moment, though, we didn't think anything of it.

Back to Basics

My rich friend Fenton Quagmire sprawled his lanky form in his Ponzi chair and propped his Mastro Antonio–clad feet on his Geppetto desk. Outside the glass cube of a building and far below on the streets the citizens of the city went to and fro, their ears affixed to cell phones.

"I'm going back to basics," Quagmire said. "Actually, I've never been to basics, so I guess I shouldn't say 'back.'"

I thought the idea of going back to basics was great. To tell the truth, I've always thought it rather disgusting to go camping in that luxurious motor home of Quagmire's, with every little comfort right down to humidity control.

"So what are we taking camping instead?" I said. "Your old two-hundred-thousand-dollar model, with just a wide-screen TV instead of the home theater?"

"Nope. Not taking any motor home at all. We're going to rough it."

"Wait a minute," I said nervously. "You're not talking tent, are you?"

"Not even a tent. You don't seem to understand. I'm getting into the real basics here."

"You mean like a plastic tarp and a couple of sleeping bags?"

"I was thinking more along the lines of a lean-to we'd make out of sticks and branches. We'll sleep in a couple of wool blankets, one each."

"Blankets! That's good. For a moment there, I thought you might want a buffalo robe."

"Wow, a buffalo robe! Where do you think we might come up with buffalo robes?"

"Probably on the Internet. It seems to have just about everything."

"Naw, not the Internet. Even though I've made a large fortune there, I want to get totally removed from technology. Blankets will have to do."

"Good," I said, "I'll start weaving mine right away."

I was fairly sure Quagmire was putting me on; either that or his train of thought had been seriously derailed. Admittedly, I myself was getting a little tired of the advances in technology. It used to be that all the different kinds of wackos sat out in their little isolated cabins or apartments somewhere. Each went through an entire lifetime without seeing another wacko of his particular ilk. Now a wacko can get on the Internet and find the other nine wackos in the world who are just like him. Then they form a club and try to figure out some way to blow up something.

Back when I was a kid we had a couple of wackos who lived in little run-down cabins back up against the mountain. I'll call them Clem and Irv. They were generally thought to be harmless, and I think they were, but I was a little afraid they might join together and cause some trouble. But one day I was talking to Irv, and he told me, "Stay away from that Clem, he's a wacko!" You just never know.

But I digress. Quagmire clearly was no wacko, but his concept of getting back to basics made me nervous.

"You remember what Thoreau wrote?" Quagmire said.

"As I recall, he wrote quite a lot," I said.

"Yeah, well, I didn't read the whole book, but I remember that one quote about why he lived in his little shack on Walden Pond. It went something like this: 'When my time comes to die, I don't want to discover that I have not lived.'"

"And his point was?"

"I don't know. I think it had something to do with his shooting a chipmunk. He cooked and ate it."

"I recall it was a groundhog," I said. "Probably one that saw its shadow when he dragged it out of its hole in March."

"Whatever. Anyway, my idea for this camping trip is that we just go out there and confront raw nature with the basics."

"You're making me nervous, Quagmire. I have confronted raw nature numerous times, and let me tell you, she's not very nice."

Then he told me not to worry, we were going to take his boat out to one of the islands in the lake, where, as I understood the plan, we could start getting back to basics. I figured that would be safe enough. If the weather got really bad, for example, we could always go sleep aboard his boat.

"I'll stop by the store and pick up some provisions," I said. "Yes, I realize you'll want us to cook everything from scratch. So, what's your feeling about marshmallows and wieners? You can't get any more scratch than that."

"Store!" shouted Quagmire. "What are you talking about? We have to catch our own food!"

"You mean like, say, fish?"

"That's right, fish."

"Can we at least take salt? I hate fish without salt."

"Salt is pretty basic. Yes, we can take salt."

"Good. At least I know we won't starve. With that new state-of-the-art fish finder of yours, we shouldn't have any trouble catching plenty of fish."

Now Quagmire made me really uneasy. He laughed so hard he could have got an infarction or something.

"You're joking, right?" he said at last. "Fish finder, indeed! No, my impoverished and disreputable friend, we are not taking my new fish finder or any other fish finder. We will find our fish the old-fashioned way, by studying the intricate clues nature so abundantly provides us, just as she did our forebears a dozen generations ago."

"My forebears always used fish finders," I said. "So I've never been too good at reading the abundant clues of nature. Sure, if a deer track has a tree seedling growing in it, I can figure out that the deer passed that way some time ago. But that's about it."

"My whole point exactly, don't you see?" Quagmire explained. "Modern living and technology in a mere couple hundred years have caused us to lose most of our instincts for the hunt. Thirty thousand years ago, I bet a hunter could smell if a mammoth or a saber-toothed tiger was close by."

"I could tell that by smell, too," I said. "But no matter how hard I look at a piece of water, I still can't tell if there's a fish in it."

"Exactly," Quagmire said. "Now, here's my theory. Once we have reduced ourselves to the basics, maybe all that knowledge that was passed on to us by our forebears but is hidden away in our genes will resurface. We can then put it to use again."

"Or we could take your fish finder," I said.

"Shut up and go get your blanket."

A short while later we landed at the island, despite a rough and windy crossing.

I had instantly become ravenously hungry the very moment I'd heard of Quagmire's plan to get back to basics.

Now I was much hungrier. The island, owned by Quagmire, consisted of about two hundred acres of sand, rock, and dirt, with about three-quarters of it covered with evergreens and assorted bushes.

We stood there staring at a bush covered with bright-red berries. Quagmire thumbed frantically through a manual on edible plants to see if he could identify it and determine if the berries were safe to eat.

"Oh-oh, here it is," he said. "The berries are poisonous."

"How poisonous?" I said.

"Ingestion of them results in severe hallucinations."

"I see," I said, spitting out several berries. But why I'd even be speaking to a large chicken I had no idea. Then the chicken said it thought we should start work on our lean-to. I thought that was a good idea, better than any Quagmire had come up with. Nature was already signaling rain, if large drops of water falling out of the sky were any indication.

I'm not sure exactly how our forebears arranged the sticks and boughs of their lean-tos so that they wouldn't leak. My theory is that they were just so tough they didn't even notice icy water running down the backs of their necks.

The large chicken lying next to me was still awake, or so I judged from the moans.

"Don't moan," I said. "After all, I let you have the whole fish."

"It was four inches long!"

"Four inches is a lot better than nothing."

"Shut up," the chicken said.

"By the way," I said, "have you ever seen the film *The Treasure of the Sierra Madre?*"

"I love that film! Why do you ask?"

"Because it's coming on one of the cable channels at eleven o'clock tonight."

"We can still make it home in time!" the chicken shouted. "Quick, back to the boat!"

Scarcely minutes later we were on our way to the mainland.

"Faster!" the chicken ordered. "Row faster!"

It was a good thing we hadn't brought Quagmire's forty-foot yacht. It's so much harder to row.

"So much for basics," I said.

"Shut up!" the chicken said.

People Who Hunt

I am now a person who hunts, as opposed to a hunter. A hunter is something different and, in my mind, something special.

Hunters, as opposed to persons who hunt, or PWHs, never find their hunting difficult enough. The weather is never horrible enough for them. The ground is never hard enough for them to sleep on. The snow is never deep enough for them to wade through. The mountain trails are never steep enough for them to climb. The game is never heavy enough for them to pack out. They are constantly looking for ways to make hunting more difficult.

Indeed, hunters very often go through the following sequence to improve on the difficulty of their hunts. First they switch from the modern rifle to the muzzleloader. With the exception of some exceedingly fast hunters, this limits them to one shot at any game. Then black-powder rifles also become too easy, and so they move on to bow hunting. Eventually, they go after even large and dangerous game with only their bow and an arrow, which essentially amounts to two sticks and a piece of string.

I must admit that while I was still a hunter, I went through all three phases: modern rifle, muzzleloader, and bow. Perhaps there are other phases hunters go through that I don't even know about, but I do retain a vivid memory of my last bow hunt. "Man," I said to myself, "hunting has got to be easier than this!" That was the moment I began to phase into a PWH.

As a teenager, my whole life revolved around hunting. Virtually every day of every hunting season, I hunted. I was a high school student, but I didn't view myself as a student. (Neither did my teachers, for that matter.) I viewed myself as a hunter. That was my identity.

I read all the outdoor magazines, and fantasized that I knew all of the authors: Jack O'Connor, Charlie Elliott, Ted Trueblood, and dozens of others. Eventually, I did get to know many of them personally, even though by then I was only a PWH.

One of my heroes in those years was Ed Zern, who at that time wrote an advertisement for Nash cars on the back page of an outdoor magazine. Those Nash ads were literature, as was Ed's later column, "Exit Laughing." One of the features of Nash cars was that you could lay the seats down and turn them into a bed. Ed had a lot of fun with that feature. As a teen, I, too, thought this a wonderful invention. Any hunter, in my opinion, would be delighted to be able to turn his car seats into a bed, particularly after a hard day in pursuit of game.

Many years later, Ed Zern and I and a friend of ours named Buck Rogers spent an afternoon in a motel room exchanging hunting stories and sipping martinis. It was one of the great afternoons of my life, despite the fact that I couldn't find my motel room afterward. Ed and Buck were still hunters, but I was only a PWH by then. Of course, I didn't let on to either Buck or Ed that I was such a person. If you're very careful and know what you're doing, you can still pretend to be a hunter, at least in a motel room while sipping martinis.

Back when I was still a hunter, I also read all the outdoor catalogs. One of my favorites was *Herter's*. I think Mr. Herter wrote all the copy for his catalog, and he didn't pussyfoot around in regard to the confidence he had in each of his products. He simply said it was the best in the world. So I bought the product, whether it was pipe tobacco or a tent or a canoe, and I never found a single reason to disagree with Mr. Herter's assessments. Perusing the contents of *Herter's* catalog one by one, and by "perusing" I mean studying them as if there were going to be a test, pretty much identified you as a hunter.

Most of my friends are either hunters or people who hunt, so I have had plenty of opportunity to study both species. People who hunt are often skilled and knowledgeable in many matters related to the outdoors, but here's the difference: People who hunt sometimes have hobbies, such as golfing or stamp collecting or woodworking, some such thing far removed from hunting. I myself, for example, have even read books not related to hunting. There are also people who think of themselves as bankers, account executives, writers, actors, or whatever, who are also PWHs. Hunters think of themselves only as hunters.

A friend of mine is a bank president, for example, but if you ask him to identify himself, he'll say he's a hunter. He thinks of himself primarily as a hunter. His job as a bank president is merely a means of supporting his hunting. His business associates are merely part of the support group for his hunting. He refuses to hire another hunter for his bank, because, he says, the two of them would spend all their time talking hunting, and never get any work done. So he would eventually have to fire the other hunter, and he doesn't want that on his conscience.

I will give you an example of the difference between a PWH and a hunter. One time Jim Zumbo and I were hunting antelope, and with a single spectacular shot I stopped the head-on charge of a crazed pronghorn. At the time I had already become a PWH, whereas Zumbo, of course, was a hunter, still is a hunter. Do you think that Zumbo would utter so much as a little amazed "wow" at the shot he had just witnessed? He did not. He raised not a single eyebrow. That is because Zumbo is a hunter. He simply expects you to make that kind of shot. That is the downside of hunting with a hunter.

On another occasion, I shot a double on chukars. (You may scoff, but it's true.) Unfortunately, both of the witnesses to this mir . . . to this superb shooting were both hunters. As with Zumbo, neither of them raised an eyebrow. Nor did they delight our companions that evening with an enthralling account of the great shot they had witnessed me make. I sat around all evening acting modest while I waited for them to relate the tale. My modesty turned out to be a total waste.

Here, on the other hand, is a definite advantage to hunting with hunters. They actually like to dress out wild game. I will do it, of course, if I am alone or with another PWH, but it is not one of my main joys in life. If you are hunting with a hunter, you never have to worry about dressing out your game. Hunters love this sort of thing. When I was hunting with Zumbo and shot that crazed pronghorn, I thought, *Well, now comes the gushy part.* I started to pull my knife out of its sheath. At that moment, Zumbo stepped forward and said, "Let me get that for you." Three minutes later the antelope was dressed out and in the back of my SUV. By then I almost had my knife out of its sheath, but what the heck.

Even though I hunted every day of every hunting season

back when I was a kid and still a hunter, as opposed to a PWH, one day in particular stands out. I got up at four and was pleased to see an icy rain pounding down outside. I put on my brand-new red felt hat, along with my other hunting togs, and started out. I crossed through the various farms between me and Greenhorn Mountain, and then I climbed clear to the top of the mountain, where I got into snow up to my knees, which was not quite deep enough but almost sufficient to satisfy me. Then I worked my way back down the mountain in the dark and icy rain, and finally walked all the way back home. The only thing that would have improved that day, to my mind back then, was if I had seen a deer. When I stepped into our kitchen, my grandmother almost fainted. The red dye in my new hat had washed down over my face, and Gram thought I'd shot myself in the head. That capped off an absolutely perfect hunt, back when I was still a hunter.

One day when I was starting to get old and grizzled, I was rushing up a steep mountainside through the snow, hoping to intersect the retreat route of a herd of mule deer. The thought suddenly occurred to me, *Wow, I can still do this!* It felt really good. Until the following morning. Not long afterward I became a PWH.

Even though I no longer qualify as one, I'm glad there are still hunters out there. In fact, I wouldn't be surprised if this fall, on a day when a bitter wind is whipping down off the mountains and there is an ominous chill in the air, a little band of hunters will set out armed with the minimum, maybe only a sling and a couple of rocks. I would love to accompany them, if only I were still a hunter.

For Every Smell,
a Nose

I had been standing at the window watching the wind build a snowdrift across the driveway when my wife, Bun, walked in and interrupted me.

"You've been standing there staring out the window all morning," she ranted. "What you need to pull you through February is a hobby of some kind."

"In February, staring out the window is my hobby," I explained. "When I started watching that drift it was only an inch high. Now it's up to nearly four inches."

"I don't know why you can't be like other husbands and lie on the couch and watch basketball all day."

"That's Retch's hobby," I said. "If I did the same hobby as Retch in February, we wouldn't have anything to talk about."

"So you're going to tell him about your snowdrift? That will keep him hanging on your every word."

"Look," I said, "it's February, a totally useless month. You can't fight February. It'll beat you every time. So what you gotta do is just let it slip by and try not to draw any attention to yourself. You know, Bun, there are some things so depressing they can just wear you down to the nubbins."

"Tell me about it."

"I am telling you about it, and February is one of the worst things for that."

"Well, why don't you and Retch go ice fishing, something that will get you out of the house. It'll do me good."

"Naw, I'm bored, not crazy. You know what February would do to me if it caught me outside?"

Just then the phone rang. It was Retch Sweeney.

"What you doin'?" he asked.

"Well, I've been trying to watch a snowdrift," I said, "but Bun keeps bothering me. You?"

"Basketball. But the reason I was able to tear myself away from watching Whatchamacallit play that other team is I got a call from Mort Finch's wife, Sally, and she said she is really worried about Mort. February has got him down pretty bad. They even brought in a psychiatrist of some kind, but the shrink says Mort is so deep in depression he's not responding to treatment."

"What's the treatment?"

"Something called aromatherapy. You ever heard of it?"

"No."

"Well, it's supposed to work great on depression. The idea, I guess, is that the shrink gives the patient a whiff of each of these different smells. I guess every so often he hits a real good smell and that calls up some pleasant experience the poor dope had one time and pretty soon he gets better and comes out of the depression."

"So what kind of smells did the shrink try on Mort?"

"Sally only mentioned four or five. Let's see, there was nectar of rose, peach blossom, some kind of perfume, oh, yeah, Channel No 5 . . . !"

"Hey, there's one that evokes like the dickens for me," I said.

Bun's ears perked up. "What evokes like the dickens for you?"

"Nothing special," I said, "just some random evoking from the days of my youth."

"Anyway," Retch went on, "Sally thinks maybe you and I can help get Mort out of his depression."

"Yeah, well, we could sure do a heck of a lot better than that shrink. Aromatherapy, for pity's sake!"

An hour later, Retch and I met at Mort's house. Sally let us in. "Don't let on that I called you," she pleaded. "For all Mort will know, you just dropped in. Do you think you can help him?"

"Think?" Retch said. "Of course we can help him. You're lookin' at two pros here."

"I sure hope so. What's in the paper sack?"

"It's a professional secret," I said. "All I can tell you is, Retch and I are pretty experienced in aromatherapy ourselves."

"Really?"

"Yeah," Retch said. "Pat and me's been into smells for a long time."

Sally showed us into the bedroom. Mort was sprawled in bed amid a tangle of covers. He had apparently been lying there staring at the ceiling. We could tell February had a terrible grip on him because he had this really pained look on his face when he saw Retch and me. "Ohh, nooo," he groaned. A guy just doesn't groan like that unless he's in real pain.

"Looks like we arrived in the nick of time, Mort," I said. "This is the worst case of February fever I've ever seen."

"Go home," Mort said. "I know you guys. You've come over here to torture me."

"Certainly not," I said. "Not this time. I was right in the middle of working on my February hobby when a thought occurred to me: 'What old Mort needs to pull him through is a little aromatherapy.'"

"Aromatherapy? Forget it. That's what that other nut tried. If I never smell another rose again, it'll be too soon."

"Yeah, we heard about him," Retch said. "Let me say this: There are some guys what know their smells and some guys what don't. Pat and me are guys what do. Now, the first thing we want you to do is stick your head in this sack, Mort, and take a big whiff."

"I ain't stickin' my head in that sack and whiffin' anything!" Mort snarled.

"You are, too," Retch said. "Here, Pat, you hold the sack open while I grab Mort by the head."

"*Wharrrfff!*" Mort whiffed.

"There," I said. "Did that evoke anything for you, Mort? You feel better now, don't you?"

Mort shouted out a crude expression.

"That's right," I said. "It's horse manure. We collected some from Wilderness Outfitters' corral on our way over here. It's quite fresh, which explains the pungency."

"I guess it's fresh!" Mort choked. "My eyes are watering."

"Before we move on to the next step, Mort, is there anything you'd like to say?"

"Yes!" Mort said. "Help! Help!"

"This is no time to be clowning around," I said. "We're trying to cure you of February. Now think about it, Mort, didn't that aroma evoke anything?"

Mort was thoughtful for a moment. "Well, maybe." He sniffed a couple of times, for the aroma of horse manure had wafted about the room. "Yeah, I guess it does. I'm reminded of the trail on our pack trip up into the Bob."

He was referring to our excursion into the Bob Marshall Wilderness Area the previous summer. It had been a great trip.

Mort had been happier that week than we'd ever seen him. "Okay," he said. "I'll admit it. The horse manure evoked a good memory. But I still feel like February, and I ain't sticking my head in no more sacks."

"Oiled leather," Retch shouted out.

"Oh, yeah," Mort said. "I love the smell of oiled leather."

"Gun smoke wafting in a marsh breeze," I whispered.

Mort smiled.

"Wet dog," Retch tried.

"You bet!" Mort exclaimed.

"Hot coffee steaming up out of a thermos at dawn!"

"Hot canvas in the morning sun!"

"Outboard exhaust!"

"Pine needles!"

"Mud!"

"Burned wiener!"

"Burned marshmallow!"

"Cedar smoke!"

"Fish frying!"

"Swamp!"

"Bacon!"

"Wet wool!"

"Moldy leaves!"

"Fresh dirt!"

"Frying onions and spuds!" Mort shouted. "Burning grease!"

By the time Retch and I and Mort were finished with aromatherapy, we were throwing on our hats and coats, ready once again to strike out on some new adventure. Then we glanced out the window. It was still February.

A couple of hours later, Sally came in to check on Mort. "I guess the aromatherapy didn't work," she said.

"Naw," Mort said. "And what's worse, Pat and Retch are taking up most of the bed."

The Ordinary

The other day my friend Starr Kelso sent me an e-mail reporting that when he and his son Matt returned from a hunting trip a while back, Matt's mother asked if they had engaged in any risky activities. Starr thought about this for a moment and then replied, "Just the ordinary." Starr's question to me was about the ethics of including in "just the ordinary" the leg he broke last year in a tree-stand incident. I told him a broken leg expands the ordinary out to a reasonable length, and by all means to include it. As a matter of ethics, however, he and Matt should go over their stories beforehand, to make sure they jibe with each other. Ethics are very important when it comes to reporting back to mothers.

Starr is lucky to have a bright son like Matt, with whom he can work out details of the ordinary. I, on the other hand, have four daughters, who constantly blabbed out nonsense to their mother regarding my activities. One day I returned from a fishing trip with two of them, and their mother asked, "So, anything interesting happen?"

"Yeah!" they yelled. "Dad nearly got swept away in the river and drowned!"

"Not again!" my wife said, glaring at me.

"I was not nearly swept away!" I replied, displaying some modest agitation. "I was performing the ordinary controlled skitter, which was made even more difficult by all the screaming!"

"Why were you screaming, if it was so ordinary?"

"I wasn't screaming. The girls were screaming." They simply know nothing about the controlled skitter, even though I have demonstrated it for them several times.

The controlled skitter, for those unfamiliar with fly-fishing, is performed in the following manner. At some point, because of the depth of the water and the current, the fisherman will notice that the soles of his waders have begun to skitter along over the rocks on the bottom of the stream. Being experienced in such matters, the fisherman realizes that if he were to lift one foot and try to step back into calmer water, he would indeed fall and be swept away. So he skillfully manipulates his feet so that he steers his skitter out of the deeper and swifter water. Any experienced fly-fisher will instantly recognize the ordinariness of the controlled skitter.

But that was the trouble with my daughters. They blabbed to their mother everything they thought was out of the ordinary, as far as their father was concerned. There was that business about Bambi, for example.

Back when I was a kid first learning to hunt, I was treated as a hero if I brought home a deer. Up until that time, my family had thought of me as primarily useless. Now my success as a hunter was treated as a cause for celebration, the whole family laughing and singing and dancing around, because we would have venison to eat for the next few months. Such a response instilled in me an enormous self-confidence and the feeling that I could do just about anything. I was a person with whom to be reckoned. Then I got married and had four daughters.

Now when I brought home a deer, the daughters would all scream and cry, "Dad shot Bambi!" I would explain that this was a bully who had been pestering Bambi and taking his lunch money. But they wouldn't buy it. I'd tell them the deer had been hit by a car, and I had been rushing him to the veterinarian when he expired right there in the passenger seat. They wouldn't buy that, either.

I am happy to report that once they got older they were more than happy to eat venison, Bambi or no. By then, of course, my sense of self-worth had been totally destroyed, probably by the questions: "Why don't you just buy some hamburger? Wouldn't that be simpler and cheaper?"

In his e-mail, Starr mentioned that he and Matt had been driving on high mountain roads, the tires of their vehicle occasionally sending rocks tumbling off sheer cliffs. He wanted to know if I would put that activity in the category of the ordinary.

"By all means," I replied. "Now, suppose you have eagles flying around in the empty space down below the edge of the road. As environmentally aware individuals, you and Matt would not want the rocks to endanger the eagles. Once again, there are ethical considerations. Also, you must take the usual precautions, one of the primary ones being never to mention the road to a mother. Or to take daughters on the same road."

I recall once driving on the Pyramid Lake road, practically a four-lane highway that leads up to the start of the trail. One corner of the road deserves a little extra attention, not only because of the sheer drop-off to the floor of the canyon a couple of thousand feet below but because of the rocks that tumble down from the mountain above and accumulate on the road. A person who is not accustomed to driving in the mountains might assume that the road has been blocked by a landslide. I'm not kidding, there are people who might actually think that. I merely put the truck into four-wheel drive and shifted into low gear. That truck climbed over the rock pile as if it were nothing. I'll admit that there was some rocking back and forth, when one tire or another was climbing over one of the larger boulders, but certainly nothing that would cause the typical hunter or fisherman any concern. My wife was sitting right next to me in the cab, and I must say I never heard a peep out of her. The reason I didn't hear her peep was that my daughters were shrieking so loud she was drowned out. All I have to say is, nobody told the girls to ride in the camper bed that hangs over the cab. Sure, the rocking up there is more pronounced, but nothing out of the ordinary.

Back in those days I was doing a lot of wildlife filming for television. Because most of the stories took place far back in the mountains, I would take the girls and their mother along so we could all enjoy camping out in the mountains together. Because of the subject matter of my stories—elk trapping, for instance—we didn't have available the amenities of the developed campgrounds. Actually, there were no amenities at all. It was my philosophy in those days that amenities, like restrooms and hot showers and level ground for tents, could easily be done without. You have never heard such complaining. I, of course, was gone all day, working my camera finger to the bone, but I would return to our camp in the evening. Then I would get it from the womenfolk, all about how they were covered with dirt and the terrible things that happened if they even thought about going potty or washing up, and so on. To improve their moods I would make up songs and sing them, like: "Snakes and bears / And other scares / Are nothing to be afeared of." But nothing seemed to calm them down.

Now that all the girls have grown into adulthood, they look back on those days of "camping out" as times of enormous fun. "Why don't we all go out camping like that now?" they ask.

"No amenities," I say.

They don't look back on our ventures out to cut the winter's firewood with the same enthusiasm. Twenty-five years later they still complain. Back then, of course, they complained to their mother when we got home. I don't care how ordinary the outing was, they would have endless complaints.

"Daddy left us all alone while he went off to look for ripe huckleberries! We could have been eaten by any number of wild animals. Several cougars walked right by us, but they apparently weren't hungry. It was terrible! And Daddy said a really bad word while he was trying to start his chain saw!"

"You didn't say that one, did you?" their mother yelled at me.

"Yeah, but the chain saw won't start unless it hears that word!"

"And furthermore," the girls went on, "after we were all shaking with fear and dirty and exhausted, Daddy made us help him load the firewood! It was awful!"

"Okay," I said in my own defense, "but when we got back to town I bought you each a chocolate-dipped ice-cream cone as payment. How about that?"

"Did you bring me a treat, too?" my wife asked.

"Yeah, but I ate it. I was so upset by all the complaining, I didn't realize what I was doing."

So Starr should be grateful he has a son like Matt, a kid who understands the ordinary.

The Kind of Guy I Am

My wife, Bun, is always after me to travel with her to far-off places. Occasionally I give in, and I have to admit that at first I enjoy the museums, temples, cathedrals, exotic markets, and natural wonders of the world. By the second day, though, I start longing for my stuff. Home is where my stuff is.

I don't mean to imply that my stuff is all that wonderful. In fact, some person might even look at it and say, "You should get rid of all this junk." Aside from my wife, though, it's even possible other people would say the same thing. Hey, my stuff is very valuable, if only to me. It's the kind of guy I am.

Let's say Bun and I are sitting at a café table in St. Mark's Square in Venice. It's a pleasant fall afternoon. Crowds of beautiful Italians are surging around us, and we are surrounded by spectacular architecture and relics of ancient history. Bun has just finished her exotic cup of coffee and is soaking up the ambiance of the place. Suddenly, she gives me a stern look. "Must you keep drumming your fingers on the table?"

I haven't realized I've been drumming. I'm thinking of my stuff, specifically of my fly-tying stuff. If I had my fly-tying stuff with me, I could tie the fly I just now thought of. I'm not sure what it would imitate, but it would be lovely and it would be deadly. I would give it a deer-hair body, for flotation, and a couple of bright yellow wings, so I could see it in rippling currents. I imagine a big cutthroat drifting out from behind a rock on the Clark Fork to suck it in. He has never in his entire life seen a fly that looks like this. He's curious. He decides to give it the taste test.

The deer hair would come from a gnarled old chunk of deer hide I keep with my fly-tying stuff. I can't remember exactly which deer I took the chunk of hide from. Maybe one of those I got while I was still a teenager, out hunting with the Russell boys.

"Okay, what are you thinking about now?" Bun demands.

"Only about a fly I could tie, if I had my fly-tying stuff."

"Your fly-tying stuff is five thousand miles away! Besides, you haven't tied a fly in forty years!"

Forty years? Well, sure, that may be true. I happen to have many friends who are expert tiers, guys who have supplied me with hundreds of flies, of every make and model, all of which I take with me on every fly-fishing trip. My philosophy is: You never can tell.

Still, there is nothing like taking a big trout on a fly you've tied yourself. I remember the first fish I ever caught on one of my self-tied flies, way back when I was a kid. I'm not sure whether the fish struck the fly or whether the fly had simply scared it to death. One way or another, though, the fly was involved.

If Bun thinks I won't ever tie another fly, she is seriously mistaken about that. Why else would I have a dozen—well, okay, twenty—fly-tying books? Let her answer me that. And why do I have a subscription to a fly-tying magazine? That's right, because as soon as I get home from Italy I'm going to tie up a bunch of flies. That's just the kind of guy I am.

"We really should do the Grand Canal in a gondola while we're in Venice," Bun says. "Don't you think that would be romantic?"

"Well, sure," I agree. "Who wouldn't?"

Speaking of romance, I think I really should get a new pair of waders. The problem is how to bring up that topic with Bun. Maybe during our gondola ride. Naw! I know what she'll say: "Right, you can get a new pair of waders as soon as you get rid of all those hip boots and waders you've got out in the garage!" See, that's the problem with wives—they don't understand about stuff. You never throw stuff away. That would be like throwing away your identity.

Like all the other fishermen I know, I have a large cardboard box almost full of old reels. Probably the first reel I ever owned is in that box someplace. It would be easy to find if I simply dumped the box out onto my workbench, but one of the Laws of Stuff is that you never simply dump out. There are archaeological layers in the box. As you work your way down, you go through the various stages of your life. I know, for example, that if I worked my way down I would come to reels from my teenage years. There would be a silvery reel there that all you had to do was press a lever and it would suck in your excess line. It was an automatic reel. No fly-fisherman worth the name would be caught dead with such a reel today, but back when I was a teen, an automatic reel meant you were at the top of your game. The automatic reel was the kind of guy I was back then. I was at the top of my game. But there's no point dwelling on that.

I have a rather large collection of old metal Band-Aid boxes. There must have been a period in my life when I went through Band-Aids as if they were going out of style. In any case, I now have a collection of the little white tin boxes. They're probably antiques by now. Back in the olden days, they made perfect worm containers that fit neatly into the pocket of your shirt or vest. Some of mine still have little clumps of hardened dirt in the bottom of them. I wonder what they're worth, even though I'd never think of selling any of them. Maybe I'll pass them along to one of my grandsons in my will. Boy, won't he be tickled. He'll say, "No doubt about it, this is the kind of guy Grandpa was."

Have I mentioned my collection of snowshoes? No? Well, all right, then!

There was a time when I could have named the snowshoes by type, but now the only type I can remember is Bear Paws. During the winters of my youth, I practically lived on those Bear Paws. Because my parents had once lost their minds, we owned a herd of milk cows. Our lives revolved around those stupid cows. In the winter, blizzards would pile up drifts between the barn and the creek, so the cows couldn't get to water. *Good,* I thought. *Now they'll all die and I'll be rid of them.* But my stepfather said, "I've got an idea. You can pack water to the cows on your snowshoes." And that is what I did. As a result, I became very good on the Bear Paws. If it hadn't been for watering the cows, I could have gone on the stage and made a lot of money tap dancing on those snowshoes.

I have just about every kind of snowshoe, from sleek modern types made of aluminum and plastic to a long and well-worn pair used by our Arctic troops in World War II. Fighting a war of any kind doesn't appeal to me, but fighting a war on snowshoes seems to me to be almost as bad as watering cows on them.

Bun gives me another one of her stern looks. "What are you thinking about now?"

"Just my collection of snowshoes," I say.

"Your snowshoes! You haven't worn any of those snowshoes in ten years!"

"Just you wait until next winter," I say. "I'll show you how to tap-dance on a pair of Bear Paws."

That's the kind of guy I am.

High-Centered

(And Other Life Lessons)

It has long seemed to me that we outdoorsmen should actually learn something from our various outings, rather than simply dedicating ourselves to the rigorous pursuit of hunting and fishing (also known by wives as "out having fun"). By "learn something" I don't mean that we should come in from a fishing trip and shout out to the missus, "I just figured out the central thesis of Sartre's *Being and Nothingness*, as well as deducing the significance of gravitational waves, not that anyone cares." Rather, I think that our outdoor experiences should teach us some lessons both practical and philosophical that we can apply to our regular lives.

For example, my wife and I undertook an outing the other day. Well, in truth, we had no intention of actually being *out*. We were in our car and engaged in what might be thought of as a scouting expedition. Suddenly, our vehicle became high-centered. For those of you who don't often get off paved roads and who lack mechanical know-how, I should explain that there is this bulbous thingamabob protruding under the front of a four-wheel-drive vehicle that causes the front wheels to engage and pull you out of a spot you were seriously stupid to drive into in the first place. Not being stupid, or at least not seriously so, I right away noticed such a spot directly ahead of us. I stopped our vehicle and started to back up. At that point, my wife shouted, "Look! Is that a bear?" Having a keen interest in bears, I swiveled my head around, all the while continuing to back up. It was then that our vehicle mindlessly climbed up over a mound of earth and high-centered. I was about to step out and determine the cause of our abrupt stop, when it occurred to me that it might be a good idea to first check on the bear. As it turned out, "the bear" proved to be nothing more than a black stump. I do have a keen interest in all wildlife, including bears and black stumps. Although I have never been attacked by a bear, one dark night I did have a black stump rear up right next to me. I soon realized, of course, that it was nothing but a harmless piece of wood, but by then I was a quarter of a mile away and picking up speed.

I eventually got the bulbous thing free from the mound of dirt and we proceeded on our scouting expedition. My point (in case you are wondering) is there should be some bit of wisdom we could learn from the experience of high-centering, some nugget of knowledge that could be applied to our everyday lives. Could it not be an analogy for some predicament we are constantly getting ourselves into? I racked my brain over it for several hours and came up with nothing. But that doesn't mean there isn't some useful lesson to be gleaned from the experience. Think about it.

Back when I was a teenager, my friend Retch Sweeney and I hiked far back into the mountains north of our homes. Even though at one point we were practically dying of thirst, we chose to stay high up on a ridge, because if we dropped into the creek drainage far below, where there was plenty of water, the mosquitoes and deer flies would devour us. As it turned out, we chose to stay on the ridge. This was the wrong choice, because that night a lightning storm came up and nearly killed us. What can be learned from this experience? I've spent half a century contemplating that question and haven't come up with anything yet. But think about it.

As a youngster, I read Mark Twain's *The Adventures of Huckleberry Finn*, and from then on was fascinated with log rafts. Instead of the Mississippi River, my friend Crazy Eddie Muldoon and I had only Sand Creek at our disposal. I figured that even though we didn't have the Mississippi, a raft would eventually get us at least as far as Memphis. How far could that be from Blight City, Idaho, anyway? I don't remember how many rafts Crazy Eddie and I built, but it was quite a few. Here's the interesting thing: Whenever the time came to test the safety factor of one of our rafts, Eddie would notice that he was wearing his good pants. (What, you might ask, would be the risk to his pants in testing a log raft? Don't ask.) My own response was that I had just received an enormous stroke of good luck, from nothing more than wearing my old pants. Otherwise, Eddie would have got to test the rafts! At the time, come to think of it, all my pants were old, so I was practically wallowing in good luck. Every time I put on a different pair of pants, they turned out to be lucky. So whenever we needed to test a raft, I was wearing the right pants for the job, a pair of lucky ones. It was a good thing, too, because my raft testing usually resulted in my floating down the creek with a log under each arm. Without lucky pants, I might very well have drowned. So let this be a lesson to you. Always wear your old pants whenever there might be some risk involved in your adventure.

Several years ago I was on a hunt in Wyoming. As often

seems to be the case, I was the last hunter of our party to get his antelope. Day after day the other hunters sat around camp looking bored while I went out in search of my pronghorn. Fortunately, there was a pretty woman along on the hunt, and one day she said to me, "Pat, I know where you can find a really dumb antelope."

"That's the most absurd thing I've ever heard," I responded. "Can you draw me a map?"

She drew me a map on the back of an envelope and marked the spot with an X. I drove out to the X and, sure enough, there was the dumb antelope right where the pretty woman said it would be. As a result, I can report that a dumb prong-horn tastes every bit as good as a smart pronghorn. So the les-son to be learned from this is that anytime you go hunting in Wyoming, take along a pretty woman.

My first actual overnight camping trip took place in a wilderness area, which back then consisted of any area more than twenty feet from my back door, after dark. My friends and I were of the impression that we should take every camping item we owned: packsack, packboard, tent, sleeping bag, air mattress, pillow, extra blanket, camp stove, lantern, candles, flashlight, compass, ax, saw, jackknife, hunting knife, machete, cook kit, large iron skillet, large iron pot, and every kind of food imaginable, right down to the milk for oatmeal. My fellow campers each brought equal amounts. I don't know about the other guys, but my pack was so heavy that when I lifted my foot to take the first step I couldn't get it back on the ground—and I'm not kidding!

As the years passed and we got older and more experienced, the size of our packs diminished until they were scarcely larger than a basketball. We now moved swiftly through the forests and mountains, and often would climb several high peaks in a single day. At night we would sit around our campfire and laugh about that very first camping trip and all the stuff we hauled along. Then one of us would say, "Yeah, but we were a whole lot more comfortable back then." We would solemnly nod. Somebody might add, "Remember the meals we cooked? Wow, what I wouldn't give for one of them now!" Sadly, we would roll up in our thin blankets and, using a rock for a pillow, go to sleep.

The lesson to be learned here is that one doesn't necessarily get wiser as one gets older!

Hunting and fishing are sports of expectation. The very best hunters and fishermen are those who expect at any moment for the world's largest buck to step into view or the world's largest rainbow trout to chomp down on the lure. Wouldn't it be wonderful to live all of life with that kind of intense expectation written large over your whole being? Sure, you would get some weird looks, but other than that it would be pretty neat.

Oh, I just thought of a life lesson for high-centering. Suppose your boss comes in and says, "You got that job done yet?" You say, "No. While I was walking across the office a while ago, I got high-centered on another project." If the boss doesn't like that for an answer, think of it this way: From now on you'll have a lot more time for hunting and fishing.

A Look Too Many

My wife, Bun, gazed directly out the windshield with an icy stare. "Stop and ask directions," she said menacingly.

We were on our way to Lud Parsley's farm. Lud had invited me out to do some pheasant hunting. I had never been to the farm, but since it consists of about a million acres, I couldn't imagine I would have any trouble finding it. Heck, just drive west from my home, and I had to bump into a million-acre farm.

My dog, Clem, was in the backseat and starting to whine. I'd told him to go to the bathroom before we started, but you know how dogs are. They never listen.

"Stop and ask directions," Bun growled. "We've been driving for hours."

Back in the olden days, when we were both younger, I'd get Bun to go down into the brush and flush pheasants. She wasn't very good at it. I think the loud cursing scared the pheasants, and they'd run off without giving me a shot.

Eventually, I replaced Bun in the field with assorted dogs, the latest being Clem. I won't go into his make and model, but he can accelerate from zero to sixty in ten seconds in pursuit of the nearest songbird. (Songbirds aren't bad eating, but they're small and kind of bony.) Nowadays, Bun sits in the car and reads a book while I hunt. Clem isn't as good on retrieving, but he doesn't make snide remarks, either, if I happen to miss a shot.

"Stop and ask directions!" Bun demanded. "We're halfway to Seattle!"

"Oh, all right," I acquiesced. "I'll stop at the next farm."

I don't know what it is about wives, or maybe women in general. They're always saying, "Stop and ask directions." They know nothing about the people who give directions. Men know. They give directions themselves. That's one of the reasons men don't like to stop and ask for directions.

The next farmhouse had about thirty vehicles parked out front. It looked like either a wedding or a funeral. As it turned out, the latter was the closer guess. Unbeknownst to me, at that moment, the farmer in question, old Isaac Beuford, was on his deathbed. I learned this from the woman who answered the door, presumably Isaac's housekeeper.

"Mr. Beuford is breathing his last," she told me. "All his relatives are gathered in his bedroom, sobbing and moaning and assessing the furnishings."

"I'm sorry to hear that," I said. "I'll try the next place."

"Oh, please don't do that," she said. "Mr. Beuford would be furious with me if I turned away a gentleman requesting directions." She disappeared into the house, presumably toward Mr. Beuford's bedroom. Presently, I heard a great deal of shouting. Then came a bull-like roar, and the place fell silent. I thought maybe I should make a run for the car. A large man in a nightgown came tromping down the hallway toward me. He opened the screen door and held out his hand. "Hello," he said. "I understand you need directions. Beuford's my name."

I said, "I'm sorry to take you away from, uh, whatever you were doing, Mr. Beuford."

"Oh, don't worry about that. I was getting mighty bored with it all. Then Elsie—that's my housekeeper—said there was a man at the door who needed directions. Right away, of course, all my sons-in-law leaped to their feet and volunteered. But they're all idiots. I decided I'd best get out here and give you the directions myself. You're the first person in several years to stop and ask directions, and I simply couldn't pass up the opportunity. To tell the truth, I'm suddenly invigorated. If you have time, I'll kill a steer and we'll have us a barbecue."

"Sorry," I said. "I'm in a bit of a rush." I understood his sense of invigoration, though, because I give a pretty good direction myself. Sometimes I don't know the place the person is headed, but I don't let that stop me for one minute. It would be rude to do otherwise. "I'm headed for Lud Parsley's farm," I said, "to do a little pheasant hunting. I'm sure I could find it if I just drove around a bit more, but my wife insisted I ask directions. You no doubt recognize the circumstance, Mr. Beuford."

"I certainly do. If I was looking for the Pacific Ocean, my wife, old what's-her-name, would insist I ask for directions. It is the nature of women." He closed his eyes for a moment, as if to concentrate on the shortest route to Parsley's farm. "Okay," he said after a bit, "what you do is head west on down the highway for two looks. Then you will see a white farmhouse with a grain silo out back."

"Two looks?"

"Don't you know about two looks?"

"No, sir, this is the first time I've ever heard the expression."

Mr. Beuford smiled, obviously pleased with my show of ignorance. "Well, get back in your car and turn it to the west on the highway. Pick out some object as far away as you can see, a tree or a rock or something that won't be moving around. You pick a horse or a cow, you might never catch up with it." He chuckled appreciatively at this remark. "Then you drive to the object. That's one look. Then you pick out another object as far away as you can see and that's two looks."

"Got it," I said. "And the white farmhouse with the silo is Parsley's."

"Nope, that's Jasper Riley's place. Right across from his house is Rosebud Road. Turn on it and drive over to Dover Road. Turn right on Dover."

"How far to Dover?"

"About three looks. Then you turn right on Dover and drive down it for one look or until you come to Boulder Road. Take a left, and two looks down that road you'll come to a large brick house."

"And that's Parsley's place?"

"No, that's Ed Frick's place. Frick is a friend of Parsley's, and he'll be able to give you directions right to his farm."

I thanked Beuford.

"No problem, son. Happy to be of service." Then he shouted over his shoulder. "Elsie, round me up some clothes and my boots! I think I'll go plow a field."

When I got back to the car, Bun asked, "So, did you get directions to the Parsley farm?"

"Yes, I did."

"Now, aren't you glad I insisted you stop and ask for directions?"

"I certainly am," I said.

I figured if I just drove west a bit more, I couldn't help but run into a million-acre farm.

The Eighty

On our return from a fishing trip, Retch Sweeney suddenly asked, "You want to swing by the Eighty?"

"Gosh, yes," I said. "I haven't seen the Eighty in thirty years."

"Been a long time for me, too," he said. "I haven't been back since Uncle Albert sold the place. He's long gone, of course."

"Oh, I'm sorry to hear that."

"Hey, Tucson ain't that bad. In his nineties but fussy as ever."

Fussy? *Fussy* is scarcely the word for Uncle Albert.

During our college days, Retch and I and Tim Martin spent at least a couple of weekends of every deer season up at Uncle Albert's, hunting the Eighty. It was about a one-hundred-mile drive from the university. We slipped away early on Friday and arrived at Uncle Albert and Aunt Ethel's by six o'clock.

Aunt Ethel always had dinner waiting for us, maybe chicken stew with dumplings, for example, something we never got at the college cafeteria, which specialized in grease with strange stuff floating in it. For dessert, and Aunt Ethel always made dessert, peach shortcake, always served with mountains of homemade whipped cream.

Breakfast the next morning took about an hour. Typically, we had home-smoked bacon, scrambled eggs with herbs, hash browns grated fresh that morning by Aunt Ethel, toast cut from thick-crusted loaves of homemade bread, and endless coffee, black and very strong but smothered with dollops of fresh, thick cream.

After breakfast, Uncle Albert would take the three of us hunters into the living room and give us the Rules for hunting the Eighty. There were quite a few Rules, but I've forgotten most of them. One purpose of the Rules was to impress upon us what a great privilege it was to be hunting the Eighty. Only the Chosen Few had the honor bestowed upon them, in this case, Retch, Tim, and me. It made us feel pretty darn important.

The Eighty consisted of 80 acres, or one-eighth of a section's 640 acres. I never thought of the Eighty as a mere 80 acres, though. To me it was an endless, magical place. It was covered with larch, pine, cedar, birch, aspen, and cottonwood, to name but a few of the tree species there. For many years, Uncle Albert allowed his cows to pasture in the Eighty, but as the land gained in value to him, he apparently became offended by the cows' casual habits of personal hygiene and found somewhere else for them to graze. With the cows gone, the Eighty quickly returned to its wild state, growing among other things thick stands of new trees, which Uncle Albert referred to as "thickets."

Once he had us in the living room, Uncle Albert would assign each of us a hunting spot. He had names for all the different places. I was usually assigned to the Monument. This was a small clearing in the woods. I was to stand behind some trees and watch the clearing. There was no sign of any kind of monument in the clearing or anywhere else on the Eighty for that matter. This apparently concerned Uncle Albert not at all. Nor did the other locations. Buttercup and Wild Strawberry, to name a couple, produced not a single one of their namesakes.

One of Uncle Albert's Rules was, "No shooting sideways." This was a safety precaution, because the shooting spots were all pretty much in line with each other. Another of Uncle Albert's Rules was, "No going to the bathroom on the Eighty." He used, of course, much more basic and specific language than can be used here.

"But what if you have to go real bad?" asked Retch, whose uncle Uncle Albert was.

"Well, then you got to walk back to the house and use the bathroom. If it appears you can't make it to the house in time, you can always cross the fence and use the Griddley place." The Griddleys obviously weren't all that fussy.

One of the major drawbacks of this Rule was that as soon as you were stationed in your place, you instantly had to go to the bathroom. But you were afraid to move because the other hunters might shoot forward or backward. And there was always the risk that one of them might forget the Rule and shoot sideways. So you just stood there and suffered.

At noon, Uncle Albert came out in his pickup truck and took us in for lunch. All three of us hunters rode in the bed so as to show no favoritism. This was another of the Rules.

Aunt Ethel would have whipped up a stack of fried chicken, mashed potatoes and gravy, assorted accompaniments, and pecan pie with whipped cream for dessert. Then Uncle Albert would load us back into the truck and haul us out to our hunting places on the Eighty. In the evening he'd return to haul us in for supper, for which Aunt Ethel would have pulled out all the stops. We'd have roasted grouse, grouse gravy, mashed potatoes, green beans, asparagus spears, and upside-down pineapple cake with whipped cream for dessert.

Sometimes Uncle Albert came out and helped us with the hunting. One time I noticed a little fir tree on the other side of the Monument that I hadn't noticed before. Never having been good at noticing things, I didn't pay it much attention. But all at once I noticed the little fir tree scurrying across the Monument right at me. It was the sort of thing almost anyone would have noticed. Then the fir tree hissed at me, "Watch your thickets!" I wasn't accustomed to taking advice from little fir trees, but, nevertheless, for the rest of the day I watched my thickets. They didn't do anything.

That evening I noticed the little fir tree in Uncle Albert's woodshed. It had a Christmas-tree stand attached to the bottom of the trunk.

Tim later asked me if I had ever had a fir tree talk to me.

"No, of course not," I replied. "Why?"

"No reason," he said.

It has been a long time since I've known a person with an eighty intact. I sometimes wonder what kind of a man owns an eighty. I guess it's whatever kind of man Uncle Albert was.

All the time we were in college, we often talked about "goin' north to hunt." It impressed our fellow denizens of the dorm. To us three hunters, "north" always meant the Eighty.

Driving back from our fishing trip, Retch stopped the car next to a walled housing development.

"Why are you stopping here?"

"This is the Eighty."

"You're kidding!"

"Nope. It was a shock to me, too."

Up ahead were a gate and a sign. The sign said the name of

the place, Stone something, even though there had probably never been a stone on the Eighty. Uncle Albert would not have allowed it.

"They should have called it 'The Eighty,' " I said.

"Probably never occurred to them," Retch said.

A guard at the gate let us pass after taking down our license number and our names. Retch said the houses started at half a mil and went up from there. There was an English estate mansion on the Monument, or at least about where I judged the Monument to have been. A small herd of deer stood on the Monument gazing back at us. Then they returned to the business of devouring the remains of a hedge.

The whole Eighty was overrun with deer. There wasn't a flower or green sprout to be seen.

"The residents don't allow any hunting on the property," Retch said.

"Maybe they should have called the place 'The Deer Farm,' " I said.

"Yeah," Retch said. "All the residents hate the deer now. They can't grow a plant."

"Serves them right," I said. "Buying into a housing development on the Eighty."

"I don't know about that," Retch said. "All the years we hunted the Eighty, we never saw a single deer, not that we expected any!"

"Yeah," I said. "Aunt Ethel's meals were fantastic, weren't they?"

Performance Netting

No aspect of sport fishing is so underrated and unappreciated as the netting of hooked fish. I'll give you an example. My friend Dave Lisaius was recently fishing with another friend of his and hooked an enormous lake trout. When he finally got the huge fish up next to the boat, according to Dave, the netter botched the job and the fish got away. Dave then screamed, "I might just as well have had McManus with me!"

I seldom get any compliments from Dave, and that is certainly one I will treasure. Alas, I must point out that Dave has botched a number of nettings for me. Once, we had been fishing for kokanee at Lake Koocanusa without taking a single fish in several hours. Always impatient, I said, "To heck with kokanee. I'm going to fish for bull trout."

Dave laughed his cynical laugh. "Good luck," he said dismissively.

I tied on a Rapala and sent it hurtling toward a rocky cliff that descended straight down into the depths for about sixty feet. Scarcely had the lure made contact with the water than a large bull trout grabbed it. I skillfully played the lunging monster until at last it tired enough that I was able to work it toward the boat. Up to this point, Dave had observed the heroic struggle between me and the fish with a bored countenance.

"It's a big one!" I yelled at him. "Get the net."

He languidly arose, looked about the boat for the net, yawned, ate another Oreo, and then moseyed over to where the fish thrashed alongside the boat. He made a few jabbing motions with the net in the direction of the fish, much in the manner of a backyard chef trying to flip flaming hamburger patties on a blazing grill. Then he announced, "Uh-oh, your fish got off."

Probably I should not have accused Dave of poking the fish loose from the lure. Dave is a true sportsman and no true sportsman would do such a thing. It is just that he is not a skilled netter. The simple fact is, he catches most of the big fish and I net them. He doesn't get much netting practice. So I will forget that he failed to net my big bull trout. It has been twenty years now since that unfortunate event, and I certainly have no intention of remembering it for another twenty years, no siree.

My stepfather gave me my first landing net when I was about ten. It was a very fancy landing net, the frame curving out from the handle into a beautiful oval. It was made of two types of hardwood, a dark and a light, and had green netting. My basic method of landing fish in those days had been to flip them back over my head. Sometimes I had to climb trees to get my fish, but otherwise the method was quite efficient.

Netting fish with the new net was much more difficult. Because I had it attached to my belt, it just seemed so much more awkward to bring the fish in close enough and then go through all the contortions to scoop the net under it. Later, my stepfather pointed out that I should have attached the net to my belt with a stretch cord, which did make netting fish a whole lot easier. Another problem with the net was that my fish often dropped straight through the mesh, thereby complicating matters even further.

Over the years I have become quite expert with the landing net. Oh, the occasional angling friend will howl like a banshee whenever I fail to get his fish in the net, but that rarely happens anymore.

I should point out, for those just getting started with fishing, that the preferred method for netting a fish is to bring it into the net headfirst. This is based on the belief that fish cannot swim backward. Therefore, if the fish gets loose from the hook at the last moment, he will swim into the net and not out of it. As I say, it is the common belief of anglers that fish cannot swim backward. But here I must point out that some fish can. You may find this hard to believe, but I have observed it myself, especially with older and larger fish, who have had several years to practice. True, I have had fish swim backward out of a net only when they were of trophy size and had been hooked by Dave Lisaius. It doesn't happen often, and I must say it always shocks me to see one of Dave's fish dart away tail first.

I recently heard from Todd Smith, the editor of *Outdoor Life*, that he would be in town for a conference. He said he would come out a couple of days early so we could visit and maybe go fishing together. At first I thought I would keep Todd all to myself and set up my own little fishing trip for the two of us over in Idaho. Then I got to thinking of the little mishaps that occur on my trips, a broken bone here, a broken bone there, a treble hook embedded dangerously close to the jugular, and so I decided to call my friend Al Liere, a real outdoor writer. Al said he would be delighted to set up a trip for me and Todd. So right away he called Al Rettman, a retired schoolteacher. Al R. said he would have the boat and all the gear and tackle we might need waiting for us at a dock on Lake Roosevelt. I couldn't have been more pleased to have worked out all the arrangements so easily, but after you've been in this business as long as I have, you develop a certain talent.

True to his word, Al Rettman met us right on time at the dock, the boat already launched. During the day, we fished for walleye, rainbow trout, and smallmouth bass. It was pretty much a typical fishing trip, at least up to a certain point. The wind blew in all directions all day, so Al had to steer constantly and couldn't fish. That left Todd, Al Liere, and me to man the rods.

With great difficulty, I managed not to get a single bite all day, so that I would be left in charge of my area of expertise—netting! This, of course, was what I wanted, an opportunity to show my stuff firsthand to the editor of *Outdoor Life*.

Suddenly, Todd's rod whipped down in a manner that indicated he had a major fish on. This was what I'd been waiting for. As Todd fought the fish in toward the boat, it did occur to me that this might be one of those fish that can swim backward. Believe me, that thought raised a sizable crop of goose bumps on me. But not to worry. Presently, Todd had the fish right up alongside the boat, just as if he had done this before. I stepped forward and, using the classical swoop motion, netted the fish and brought it aboard.

The fish was a nice rainbow, in the twenty-inch range, possibly larger by now. Oddly, though, Todd failed to comment on the skill with which the fish had been netted. He has fished all over the world, and I supposed it was possible that at one time or another he had seen a fish netted with equal skill and style. I decided that to impress him at all I would have to increase the difficulty of my art and move to the utmost level—performance netting!

It wasn't long before Al Liere hooked a rainbow approximately the same size as Todd's. This was my chance. Sensing what I was up to, Al brought the fish in so that it managed to swim under and between the trolling and main motors, a netting situation that amateurs might easily think hopeless. Then the fish turned and stuck its nose barely out between the motors. The situation seemed almost impossible even to me, a master netter. Then I noticed that one barb of the treble hook was attached downward through the lower jaw of the fish. The other two barbs were outside the lip. Hesitating not a second, I thrust the net down in such a manner that it hooked the two outer barbs. I then hoisted the fish into the boat completely outside the net!

Todd was impressed. And so was Al Rettman. Apparently, neither of them had ever before witnessed performance netting.

Al Liere, on the other hand, claimed that the whole incident had to be an accident. His opinion was that I had thrust the net at the fish, missed it completely, and, in withdrawing the net, had accidentally caught it around the treble hook. His only comment was, "Weird stuff like this happens every time I go fishing with McManus!"

In response, I can only say, "Ha!"

The Pasture

There are fragrances. Beyond fragrances are smells, beyond smells are odors, and beyond odors are stenches. Beyond stenches is what I am about to write of here.

The very best fishing near our farm was a stretch of Sand Creek below the next farm over, Dub Wallace's place. It was the best fishing because it was hardly ever fished. The reason it was seldom fished was that in order to get to that particular stretch of the creek you had to cross a large pasture owned by Dub's big old Guernsey bull. On a scale of meanness this creature was off the chart. A person would have to be a fool even to think about crossing that pasture. Indeed, the first time I crossed it, The Bull nearly got me. It was then that I figured out that The Bull was ignorant of the concept of leading a moving target, in my case a target that was moving extremely fast. He always held dead-on, which gave him a curved trajectory, while I kept to a straight line, and that was my advantage.

Fortunately, there was a sturdy fence at the end of the

pasture, and I was able to throw my fishing pole over the top wire and then roll under the bottom wire. The Bull would at that instant slide to a stop at the fence, paw the ground, bellow loudly, and shake slobber from his huge muzzle. I would then pick up my fishing pole and head down to the creek. It is important for me to point out here, for those persons planning to run from bulls, that it is necessary to win the race. To come in second or even to tie at the fence does you no good at all.

The Bull would stand at the fence and glare down at me as I fished along his creek. I knew what he was thinking. He was thinking he would do just about anything to keep me from fishing his creek, even though he had never before considered fishing it himself. After a while he would get bored, and wander off to the other end of the pasture. That was when I would make the return dash home.

At the time of my first race with The Bull, I was about ten. For a few minutes in the middle of the pasture, I thought I might not get any older, and this thought increased my speed by several knots. I continued in this practice for a couple of years, until one day The Bull suddenly disappeared. This happened shortly after The Bull took offense at something Dub either said or did, at which point he and Dub did several quick laps around the pasture, with Dub losing ground at every lap. Dub eventually made it to the top of a tall stump, later claiming that he achieved the ascent in a single leap, even though anyone seeing the height of the stump would realize it must have had a ladder leaning against it. That kind of exaggeration from a farmer was considered fairly normal in those days and no one held it against him.

Even after The Bull disappeared, the stretch of creek below his pasture remained the best fishing the entire length of Sand Creek. By then I was about twelve years old and could stroll leisurely across the pasture, toss my fishing pole over the fence, and climb through the wires in a dignified manner. On the other side of the fence the ground dropped away rather sharply to the creek below. By "rather sharply," I mean that it was only a few degrees off vertical. My friend Vern Schulze and I used it as our sledding hill. It was on this hill that Vern and I experienced the most spectacular sledding crash of our young lives. I was seated behind Vern on the sled when it went out of control, and I was thrown over the top of him, at which point Vern and the sled ran over me at least once and possibly twice. Even though I wasn't hurt, every single button was ripped off my coat. If I had told anyone about that weird accident he probably would have thought it was a miracle and . . . But I digress.

The part I've been trying to get to here is that one day I was crossing the pasture and noticed a faint smell drifting out of the woods beyond. The next time I crossed the pasture, the smell had become a rather strong odor. The following week it had become a stench. The week after that it had become something way beyond stench. I'm not sure how to describe it except to say it was a malevolent force that stopped you in your tracks and then forced you back. The Thing Beyond Stench could not be penetrated. Now not even I could fish that stretch of the creek.

At the time, I was growing up in a family of women: my mother, my sister, and my grandmother. The one adult male influence in my life was an odorous old woodsman by the name of Rancid Crabtree. Rancid claimed to have taken a bath back in 1938, but he had no proof, and nobody believed it. I learned from him the importance of the hunting terms *upwind* and *downwind*. I, along with all of our neighbors, made a practice of staying upwind of Rancid. Housewives threw open the dining room windows when they saw him headed their way. (They always tried to get the windows open beforehand, because they didn't want to hurt his feelings.)

I learned other things from Rancid, too, such as how to hunt and fish and, best of all, how to act like a man.

"Stop that whining!" he'd snap at me after a hike along his winter trapline. "Course yer feet feels like thet when they's thawin' out. It jist means some of yer blood has iced up. Won't kill ya, thet's fer dang sure, lessen the ice dams up and busts one of yer erteries."

"My erteries!" I'd yell, being unfamiliar with medical terminology. I worried for years about my erteries damming up and bursting.

One day I stopped by Rancid's shack just as he came out carrying a quart jar with a lid on it. "Ha!" he said. "Ah was jist headed over to git ya. Got a little test fer ya."

"A test?" I said. "I don't want a test."

"Wahl, yer gonna take this one. Anyway, guess what?"

"What?" I said.

"Ah found us a maggot farm!"

"A maggot farm? What kind of a farm is that?"

"You wait and see. Me and you is headed over to it right now."

We were soon walking across the pasture to a little wooded area on the other side. The Thing Beyond Stench hit me full force. I staggered back.

"What's wrong?" Rancid said. "Why you stopping?"

"The stench!" I said. "I can't stand the stench."

"What stench is thet?"

Apparently, Rancid's sense of smell had long ago been destroyed. On the other hand, The Thing Beyond Stench seemed to be oozing through the pores of my skin. By now, of course, I knew what it was. Something had died back in the woods.

Rancid grabbed me by the shirt and dragged me along. As we entered the wooded area I could make out through my watering eyes the source of this olfactory obscenity, a great cavernous mound consisting of the remains of some large but unfortunate creature. In school or on the school bus, when some suspicious odor arose, some kid would always inquire, "What died?" Believe me, when compared with The Thing Beyond Stench, those innocent little noxious scents were thrust deep into the realm of the insignificant.

Rancid pointed into the cavernous side of the creature. "Look! Thar's the maggot farm Ah told you about!"

"Erp!" I replied. A billion maggots vibrated in the vast interior of the creature.

"Now, this hyar's the test," Rancid said. "Hold yer hands cupped together like this." He showed me. I cupped my hands together.

"Now scoop in thar and git us a big gob of maggots fer our fishin'."

"Noooo!" I said.

"You one of them squeamish fellers? Ah cain't stand a man what's too squeamish to scoop up some maggots! Now you scoop!"

"No, you scoop!"

"I ain't scoopin'! I got to hold the jar. You scoop!"

I scooped. It wasn't half as bad as I had imagined but still bad enough to give me nightmares for a couple of months. Rancid held out the jar. I dumped in the maggots.

"Good job! Now we got ourselves enough maggots for a whole year of fishin'."

"Erp!"

A couple of weeks passed before I saw Rancid again. He was sitting on his front porch whittling a stick, the most work I'd seen him do in a long time.

"Let's take some of those maggots and go fishing," I suggested.

"Cain't," he said. "The maggots is gone."

"Gone?" I said. "How could they be gone?"

"I'll tell you how come. A bunch of flies somehow got into the jar and ate every last one of them!"

I didn't believe that for one second. He had probably gone fishing and used them all up. Whoever heard of flies eating maggots?

"Why didn't you go up to the maggot farm and get us some more?" I said.

"Ummm, let me see now. Ah had a dang good reason but it slips maw mind at the moment."

The Thing Beyond Stench kept me from fishing that section of the creek for one whole summer. Eventually, the earth absorbed the poor dead creature, and with it went The Thing Beyond Stench, which had been a whole lot worse than The Bull. At least The Bull never prevented me from fishing the creek.

Predicament

Over lunch in a restaurant one day I started to tell Starr Kelso about one of my major predicaments. He stopped me.

"I have heard that predicament four times. I must admit it improves with each telling, but I now have it pretty well down in my memory. There's really no reason for you to exhaust yourself coming up with new variations. Besides, I have a predicament of my own to tell you about."

I could not help but be amused by Starr's suggestion that he had actually experienced a predicament. "Don't be too confident," I warned. "Predicaments are an art form. It takes years of experience to pull one off even adequately. You are still young and there's plenty of time for you to learn, particularly if you pay attention to my accounts, instead of absently munching your fries and staring out the window."

"Well, I'm not sure if this experience counts as a predicament," he said, "but I thought I would run it by you, to get your expert opinion."

"Go ahead," I said, munching a fry and staring out the window.

His predicament went like this: Starr has a teenage son still at home, Matt by name, and the two of them went out bow hunting for elk a couple of years ago. As was their practice, and that of most bow hunters, they spent a good deal of time hiking away from the slightest clue that even one other person existed on the planet. The question might arise as to why bow hunters never consider the problem that if they do get an elk they will have to pack it all the way back to civilization. Packing out an elk, by the way, should be undertaken only by young bow hunters, because they will be old and senile by the time they get it to their truck.

After several hours of hiking into the wilderness, Starr and Matt arrived at a blowdown, acres and acres of trees that a mighty wind had left heaped in massive piles. As Starr described it, "The place looked like a gigantic version of Pick Up Sticks." Nevertheless, they started wending their way over rows and through piles of dead and rotting timber, even though the blowdown was close to impenetrable—in other words, perfect elk habitat. Somewhere toward the middle of the blowdown, they came upon a lone tree rising into the heavens.

Instantly, I became alert to the possibility of a predicament. As a youth, I could not pass a tree without attempting to climb it and see if I could fall and break one or more body parts. Starr, on the other hand, remained a mere beginner in the art of predicament. I could scarcely hope he would have the good sense to make some use of the tree. But I had underestimated him.

"So," Starr went on, "I told Matt that I'd climb up and see if I could find a suitable place to install my tree stand."

I was impressed. Despite the fact that Matt could have gone up and down the tree like a squirrel, Starr decided to haul his two-hundred-plus pounds up to the tip-top, his theory possibly being that the young man probably wouldn't know how to climb a tree properly. Upon reaching the uppermost regions of the tree, Starr took a firm grip on a branch and leaned out to survey the blowdown for elk. It was at this point that he discovered the branch wasn't attached to anything.

For the observer, it may seem as if the falling person arrives at his landing spot in a mere fraction of a second. For the fallee, however, there is a great deal of time to think. Mostly what he thinks about is how much this is going to hurt. In Starr's case, it hurt a great deal, quite a bit more, in fact, than Starr had considered possible. It quickly became obvious that he had broken a leg.

Breaking a leg far back in the wilderness would be a sufficient predicament for almost anyone, but Starr would not let it go at that. He had to improve upon it.

"So now there was nothing I could do but send Matt off alone to bring back help. If you can even imagine this, my very survival now depended upon a teenager."

Having had four teenagers of my own, I could easily appreciate the horror of the situation. Upon reaching civilization, would Matt call his girlfriend to apprise her in detail of his mission and the numerous obstacles he had overcome in carrying it out? Would he stop by the arcade for a few video games? Meet some of the guys at Gert's Gas 'n' Grub for a few snacks? Would he in the course of all of this forget where he had left Starr? "I know he was beneath a tree. Look for a tall tree." Those are but a few of the thoughts that might course through a father's mind while he lies at the foot of a tree awaiting a rescue force alerted to the predicament by his teenage son.

"That is as good a predicament as I've ever come across," I told Starr. "Now I think you should leave it alone. It's perfect. All you need now is a snappy close."

"Oh, no, I'm just getting started," Starr replied. "There's more."

"More?" I said.

"Yes, much more."

Soon, daylight began to fade. Still no sign of any rescuers. As Starr lay there helpless and in pain, contemplating the approach of night, two grizzlies, a pack of wolves, and a Sasquatch walked by, all of them noticing him but apparently saving him for a late-evening snack. A harvest moon rose behind the mountains and several stars appeared in the sky. And then, at long last, here came Matt, followed by a search-and-rescue team and also a man and his son, passersby who had run out of gas on the road and decided to join up for the adventure. That, by the way, is the nature of men. There is nothing they enjoy more than a good search. Rescue can be a major nuisance, but the search is wonderful.

"That's great, Starr," I said. "Now leave it there. Maybe end with, 'Boy, was I ever glad to see those guys!'"

"I can't," he said. "I'm not even to the best part yet."

From my own considerable experience with search-and-rescue teams, I should mention that when it comes to a predicament, one worth telling about, there is nothing better than to inject S&R into the situation. These lads, and occasionally lasses, will introduce a comic element that is otherwise almost impossible to achieve.

Matt, wise beyond his years, had neglected to mention to the search-and-rescue guys that his father weighed two-hundred-plus pounds. They rolled him onto the stretcher and, with bulging muscles and protruding eyeballs, lifted the stretcher to their shoulders, one man on each corner. Even in pain, Starr could not help but be amused by their agonized grunts. Now all they had to do was haul him out of the impenetrable blowdown, up and around assorted mountains, and in

and out of a few drainages, by which time they might be able
to see civilization far off in the distance.

"I don't recall much about the trip out," Starr said, "except
I do remember that one of the passersby had a shoe sucked off
in the swamp."

"Swamp!" I cried. " You never mentioned a swamp before.
A person can't just up and throw in a swamp anytime he finds
use for one."

"Maybe it was only a bog," he said. "Anyway, the guy got
his shoe sucked off in the mud and had to limp along half-
barefooted."

I had to admit that was a nice touch. "So search and rescue
managed to get you out okay," I said, waiting for the wrap-up.

"Oh, I'm not to the fire engine yet."

"What? There was a fire engine?"

"Yeah! When we finally got to the road, the S&R guys
were practically walking on their knees, some of them probably worse off than I was. But they still had to get me up to
the ambulance. There was a sheer rock cliff directly ahead of
us, with a high steep slope on both sides of it. I could hear the
S&R guys muttering to themselves, and the gist of the muttering was that they didn't want to lug me up either of the steep
grades. I tried to put in my two cents' worth, but they were ir-
ritable and wouldn't listen to me. Worse, they seemed to have
developed a deep prejudice for people who break legs far back
in the wilderness. Then one of the S&R guys comes up with
an idea."

"Stop right there," I said. "Don't tell me you actually listened to an S&R guy's idea."

"I didn't have any choice but to listen. He said, 'We could
use the hose to haul him up the cliff.' "

"Might work," said their leader. "Let's give it a try."

"Might?" Starr said. "What do you mean, *might*?"

As Starr explained, the fire engine had a hose connected to a power roller. One of the S&R guys climbed up and released the clutch on the roller and dropped a length of the hose over the cliff. They fastened the end of the hose to Star's stretcher.

"Wait a minute!" Starr yelled at them. "Stop! I think we need to discuss this!"

The S&R leader signaled the guy at the truck. An engine started. Slowly the hose began to tighten. The stretcher inched up off the ground. Starr began to rise up the cliff. He could hear the engine straining. Then it stopped. Starr was now suspended halfway up the cliff. Far down below, he could hear the S&R guys and the two passersby discussing the situation. It was decided that it would be a bad idea to throw out the clutch on the hose roller because then Starr would crash back to the bottom of the cliff and maybe break his other leg. Or they could simply drive the truck down the road a ways and drag Starr up over the top of the cliff. Somebody nixed that idea, too. (Starr thinks he was the one who objected.) Finally, the S&R guys got the engine started again and raised Starr the rest of the way up to the road. An ambulance carted the patient off to the hospital.

As an expert in such matters, I could not have been more impressed. "Do you have a name for this predicament?"

"I call it The Time I Broke My Leg," Starr said. "Matt calls it The Time I Saved My Father's Life!"

"Teenagers!" I said.

"Yeah."

Dalliance

Mr. and Mrs. Gibbons were reading the Sunday *Seattle Times* at the table in their sunroom. A faint mist drifted down outside. Like most Seattle residents, the Gibbons thought of mist as "sunshine."

Carlita, the maid, attired in a short black dress and a crisp white apron, came in with tea, eggs Benedict for Mrs. Gibbons, and scones and orange marmalade for Mr. Gibbons.

"Ahh!" said Fred Gibbons. "Warm scones. I love warm scones with orange marmalade. Thank you, Carlita."

Dorthea peered over her paper and half-glasses and said curtly, "That will be all, Carlita."

Carlita gave a little bow and left.

Dorthea dug into her eggs Benedict. Fred hated eggs Benedict. He hated even to watch someone else eat eggs Benedict, particularly his wife. He concentrated on buttering his scone. A precise and tidy man, he buttered with great care, as if restoring a Rembrandt. He was pale and soft in the face, and his carefully trimmed dark-brown hair seemed to emphasize the paleness and softness.

"What about the *Dalliance?*" Dorthea said abruptly, dabbing eggs Benedict from her lips with a linen napkin.

It was about the tenth time that week that Dorthea had mentioned the boat. Fred was too polite to think of his wife as nagging. She did do a great deal of reminding, however.

"What about it, exactly?" Fred asked, carefully concealing his irritation.

"Well, how much is that man behind in his payments?"

"About a hundred and fifty."

"Thousand."

"Yes. One hundred and fifty thousand."

"So, when are you going to take the boat back?"

"Soon," Fred said. "I have the papers made out."

"Tomorrow is soon," Dorthea said. "A week from now is not soon."

"It's kind of sad," Fred said. "After his wife died, he sold everything he owned and poured it into the boat."

"Not your problem," Dorthea said. "That was my father's boat. Papa never took it out but he still kept it in perfect condition. Why he ever wanted the *Dalliance* in the first place is beyond me. And such a silly name for a boat! But there's no reason for us to carry that Pierson fellow simply because he's run out of money."

"Ike Pierson," Fred said. "He lives on it, you know. It's his home. He's quite old."

"Yes, I do know. Old people can be rather messy, too. He's probably made a mess of it. You have to deal with this, Fred. Tomorrow! Bertie will be finished with law school in a few years and maybe then you can let him handle the difficult stuff. But for now, you still have to do it."

Fred doubted his son would ever get to law school. Bertie

hated even the thought of it. But maybe he would be good at taking boats away from old men. That would please his mother, although probably not as much as law school would.

The next day Fred drove north the sixty miles from Seattle to the marina at Anacortes. He found Ike Pierson on the aft deck of the boat. The old man was shirtless. He was sitting on his haunches, paintbrush in hand, touching up some trim with varnish. His hair was white and wild and hung down to his deeply tanned shoulders. For his age, Fred thought, Pierson appeared surprisingly fit and limber.

"Ahoy there, Mr. Pierson," he called out. He felt foolish saying "Ahoy."

"Ahoy there yourself, Mr. Gibbons," the old man said, straightening. "C'mon aboard. Well, I guess it's not up to me to be inviting a man aboard his own boat. I suppose you have the papers there in your briefcase."

"I'm afraid I do," Fred said. "I'm so sorry about this."

"Don't be," Ike Pierson said. "It's not your fault. You carried me a whole lot longer than any banker would, I can tell you that."

"I guess," Fred said. "But this boat has been your home."

"And a darn fine one, too," Pierson said. "But you don't have to worry about me, man. I've been poor before. I know how to be poor. I figure I'll get me a little place over in Spokane, something within walking distance of a library. And a grocery store. I like to read." He gave a little laugh. "And eat!"

Fred smiled. "Spokane?"

"I think maybe. Spokane is a good place to be poor. The fishing is good, too. And I won't have to look at the damn ocean. You fish, Mr. Gibbons?"

"Fish? No, no, I don't fish." Fred felt embarrassed not to have fished.

"Well, let's get them papers signed," Pierson said. "I know you're a busy man. Can't be wasting all day with an old fool like me. And I got to get started packing up."

"I'm in no hurry," Fred said. "I kind of hate to admit this, but I've never been on the *Dalliance* before."

"No! You've never been on the *Dalliance* before? I have to tell you, Mr. Gibbons, that is a mortal sin. Here, I'll give you a little tour. You're in for a treat."

Much to Fred's surprise, it was a treat. There were two state-rooms, each with its own bath and shower. The *Dalliance* could sleep six comfortably, up to eight if they were on exceptionally good terms with one another. Off the galley was a combined dining area and lounge. Even a person as fastidious as Fred would have been hard-pressed to find a smudge or a speck of dust anywhere. Chrome, brass, and polished teak gleamed on all sides.

The bridge was a glowing mystery of electronics. Pierson tried to explain the navigation system, but finally said simply, "Pick out a spot anywhere in the world and it will take you there."

"Really? Anywhere in the world?"

"That's right. Well, shoot, I might just as well take you on a little cruise. Give you some idea of what a dream the *Dalliance* is. What say, Mr. Gibbons?"

"Gosh, I . . . I guess that would be all right. Not too far out, though."

The twin engines rumbled to life somewhere below them. Ike deftly backed the boat out of its slip. Moments later they were in the open water of the bay. Gulls swooped noisily around them as if in gleeful celebration of Fred's maiden voyage on the *Dalliance*.

"Shucks," Pierson said after a bit. "We might as well put

out a rod, just poking along the way we are. Might catch us a salmon. Here, take the wheel, Mr. Gibbons."

"Oh, no, I better not . . . !"

Pierson let go of the wheel and called back as he headed down to the deck, "Just hold her steady and on line with that point across the way, Mr. Gibbons."

Fred seized the wheel in a death grip. He steered straight ahead, hoping nothing would get in his path. Like, say, a ferry! He took a quick glance back over his shoulder. Pierson, his white hair streaming out in the breeze, was baiting a large and deadly-looking hook. Then he swung the line and the string of flashers out into the wake of the boat. He inserted the rod into a holder and returned to the bridge. Relinquishing the wheel, Fred felt an odd twinge of reluctance.

Scarcely ten minutes later, Pierson roared out, "Fish on!"

Fred almost jumped out of his skin.

"Go grab the rod and start reeling!" Pierson ordered.

"No!" gasped Fred. "You do it!"

"Can't! Got some tricky waters here! You have to do it!"

Fred scrambled down the ladder and grabbed the rod out of its holder.

"Haul her back hard!" Pierson commanded from the bridge. "Then reel like crazy!"

Fred hauled back hard. The force of something wild and powerful surged through the rod and into his hands and arms. His heart leaped in his chest. He froze, half in fright, half in awe.

"Reel!" screamed Pierson. "Reel!"

That evening they took the dingy into a rocky beach and Pierson splayed the salmon out with willows and cooked it Indian-fashion over a driftwood fire. They ate the salmon with ice-cold beer. The salmon tasted so good it brought tears to Fred's eyes.

"The smoke," he explained.

Pierson smiled and nodded.

Back on the boat, Pierson suggested it might be better if they stayed anchored for the night. "We can head back in the morning."

"I suppose that would be all right," Fred said. He pulled out his cell phone. "I'll call Mrs. Gibbons and check with her."

"Great Scott, put that thing away!" yelled Pierson. "Two things never allowed on a fishing boat—bananas and cell phones! Been the rule ever since Noah launched the Ark!"

"Sorry," Fred said. "I'll call Mrs. Gibbons in the morning. From the marina."

"Good idea," Pierson said. "About tomorrow, Fred—you don't mind if I call you Fred, do you?—well, I've been thinking we might run across to Vancouver Island in the morning. We could have breakfast at the Empress in Victoria. You could call Mrs. Gibbons from there."

"Yes, by all means, breakfast at the Empress! I recall they serve a very good scone there."

"Say, Fred, you ever been to the Queen Charlottes?" Pierson asked. "They're spectacular."

"The Queen Charlottes? No, I'm afraid not."

"They're islands sort of up by Ketchikan. You know what? We could run up the Inland Passage and be there in a few days."

"Gosh, Ike, that sounds like a terrific adventure. But I really don't think . . ."

Five years slipped by, during which Dorthea divorced Fred for desertion. She had by then married a banker, a decent, steady, levelheaded man, unlike her ex. Fred still occasionally sent her postcards from various ports: Ketchikan, San Diego, Cabo San Lucas, Puerto Vallarta, Acapulco, Rio de Janeiro, and so on.

Dalliance

One day Carlita came in with a letter from Rio. It contained a brief note from Fred and a couple of snapshots. Carlita looked at the pictures over Dorthea's shoulder.

Fred was seated in a deck chair on the *Dalliance*, holding a fishing rod. His hair was long and gray now, but it contrasted nicely with his skin, which was shiny with either sweat or oil, and the color of hickory nuts. He wore only a broad grin, a pair of cut-off jeans, and a folded bandanna around his head. He appeared extremely trim, fit, and happy.

"Meester Geebons!" Carlita cried. "He's so handsome!"

"He looks like a pirate!" Dorthea snapped. "Which he is." She was referring to several savings accounts Fred had cleverly cleaned out before she could get to them. Leaning forward, she examined the picture more closely. "Carlita, can you make out what on earth is that little red thing protruding in from the edge of the photo?"

Carlita squinted at the picture. "Es a toe!" she exclaimed. "A leetle beeg toe! Has red nail polish on eet!"

"Good heavens!" Dorthea gasped. "I would never have suspected such a thing. Imagine that—Ike Pierson!"

Carlita smiled. She didn't think the toe belonged to Ike Pierson.

Another five years slipped away.

One morning Dorthea received a phone call from a man who said he was an official at the American embassy in Chile. The official informed her that Fred had died of a heart attack while fighting a swordfish. Dorthea was shocked. "Why on earth would Fred be fighting a swordfish?" she shouted at the official. "He can barely swim!"

The official informed her that a Mr. Ike Pierson had said he would be returning the Gibbonses' boat to Anacortes.

It was a couple of months later that Bertie Gibbons, now rapidly approaching middle age and long ago having given up any thoughts of becoming a lawyer, marched down the dock at Anacortes. As he approached the *Dalliance*, he noticed a tall, slender man standing on the aft deck. The man's white hair streamed out in the breeze as he watched Bertie approach. Bertie was pudgy and soft and pale, just like his father had once been, only more so. He brought with him a briefcase and a frown.

"Come to get the boat, did you?" the old man called down to him.

"Yes, I have," Bertie said sternly. "And it's about time, I must say."

"Indeed it is. Well, come aboard, man, it's your boat."

"All right," Bertie said. "Actually, I've never been on it before."

"Never been on the *Dalliance*? Oh, how can a man live with a sin like that on his conscience! We must correct that grievous error immediately!"

After a tour, the two of them sat down at the table in the lounge. Bertie was surprised to see that the old man had gone to some trouble to prepare a rather elegant tea for them. He wasn't nearly the monster his mother had described. It was certainly a relief to have the *Dalliance* surrendered in such a civilized manner. The conversation was most pleasant. The afternoon slipped away almost unnoticed by Bertie. He sipped his tea thoughtfully as he listened to the old man relate various adventures. Then he said, "Tell me again about the Queen Charlottes. How long would it take us to cruise up there through the Inland Passage?"

"A couple weeks. Three, tops. By the time we get back, you'll be handling the *Dalliance* like a seasoned skipper."

"It sounds wonderful." Bertie took out his cell phone. "I'll call Mother and see what she thinks."

"Good lord, man! Put that away! Two things never allowed

on a fishing boat—bananas and cell phones! Been the rule ever since Noah launched the Ark."

Bertie laughed and put the phone back in his jacket.

"Good," the old man said. "Now, if you're not going to eat the rest of that scone, pass it over. Along with the marmalade, if you please."

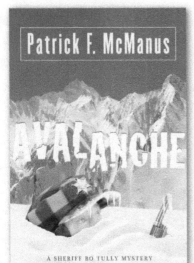